HERTFORDSHIRE DIALECT AND COUNTRY SAYINGS

EDITED BY MARGARET WARD

Margaret Ward

COUNTRYSIDE BOOKS
NEWBURY BERKSHIRE

First published as
Hertfordshire Heritage
in 1948
by John Green & Co

This expanded edition published 2003
© Margaret Ward and the estates of
Mary Carbery and Edwin Grey, 2003

COUNTRYSIDE BOOKS
3 Catherine Road
Newbury, Berkshire

To view our complete range of books,
please visit us at
www.countrysidebooks.co.uk

ISBN 1 85306 829 2

Produced through MRM Associates Ltd., Reading
Typeset by Techniset Typesetters, Newton-le-Willows
Printed by Woolnough Bookbinding Ltd., Irthlingborough

Foreword

Two centuries ago, every June, the sweet smell of Hertfordshire's fresh-cut hay was wafted on the breeze to scent the streets of London. When Archibald Jackson described haymaking in East Hertfordshire 'before the age of machinery' for the writers Edwin Grey and Mary Carbery in the 1940s, he could still recall the way the hay was cut and dried 'with the scythe an' the rake' in his day. In the words of this old countryman, the hay then was 'sweet an' dry an' green as 't should be, an' full o' seed an' Jeune flowers'.

The age-old rhythms that still moved through Hertfordshire country life in the 1940s have for most of us now passed silently into history, though they still live on in some quiet villages and hamlets. Once there was a time for everything from ploughing to sowing to harvest, and life was lived according to the seasons and the church calendar. Harvest time is recalled in some detail in this book, from the blowing of the harvest horn that called the men to work, to the pleasures of the harvest-home supper.

What has all this to do with a collection of words and sayings? When Edwin Grey and Mary Carbery collaborated on the book called *Hertfordshire Heritage* in 1948, they felt that the dialect words and country sayings that were an integral part of that old way of life and which were still in everyday use in parts of Hertfordshire were gradually being lost to future generations. They were right, too; there must be many now living in the county who have never heard the 'clear, deliberate enunciation' or the 'musical, lilting intonation' that used to characterise the true Hertfordshire countryman or woman – perhaps many who have never realised that this county has its own dialect at all.

To Grey and Carbery, the history of Hertfordshire's language and great English literature were intertwined, so that an uneducated country labourer might speak a language that Shakespeare or Chaucer would have recognised:

'We remember with pride that Chaucer wrote his immortal poetry in the East Midland dialect to which our words belong. Shakespeare's plays are sprinkled with the homely phrases and words which our Hertfordshire shares with his Warwickshire. Spenser, that great champion of dialect, borrowed them. We find them on every page of the first Bibles to be written in English: by Wycliff, 1382, and by Tyndale and Coverdale, 1525-35, both of these in the literary English

of the time of Henry VIII. Later on we come across both words and expressions in The Pilgrim's Progress, *1768. Our neighbour, Bedfordshire, shared our dialect and her great son, John Bunyan, used it freely.'*

They were not the only ones in the late 1940s and 1950s who feared that the old Hertfordshire would soon be lost forever. Sir William Beach Thomas, writing in 1950 (*Hertfordshire*, Robert Hale), rejoiced that 'you can scarcely walk a mile anywhere without enjoying some sense of the rich continuity of its wholly English character', but ended his book with a hope that 'the new satellite towns and green belts and housing estates being dumped on the county by those little interested in its special charms' would not succeed in crushing its peaceful countryside. The government's Greater London Plan of 1944 had proposed building three arterial roads through the county and three new satellite towns, with work starting at Stevenage in 1946. The outcry that greeted this assault on the countryside is mirrored today by the response to government proposals that will cover yet more acres of Hertfordshire's countryside with housing and concrete.

Now, more than fifty years later, there is nationally a new interest in local dialect and regional accents have achieved respectability. It seems high time that Hertfordshire laid claim to its own history once again, and to bring back to life for a new generation the dictionary of Hertfordshire words and sayings that Grey and Carbery put together in 1948.

The two authors were born into a very different time and place and died soon after *Hertfordshire Heritage* was published, Mary Carbery in 1949 and Edwin Grey in 1955. Both were Hertfordshire bred and lived in the Harpenden/St Albans area of the county, and both had a great love of the county and its 'folk', with a sympathetic curiosity about the everyday life of the past. This was the only book they produced together, but Edwin Grey's memories of life in the 1860s and 1870s in Harpenden, *Cottage Life in a Hertfordshire Village* (first published 1934 and reprinted 1977 and 1981 by the Harpenden Local History Society) has become a classic in local history. Mary Carbery's own account of her childhood at The Pré just outside St Albans has also been published by the Harpenden Local History Society under the title *Happy World* (1991).

The chapters of children's history that began the original *Hertfordshire Heritage* have been left out of this revised edition. The 'List of Words', however, has been extended and greater care has been taken over the cross-referencing – it might not have occurred to a reader searching for the meaning of the phrase *declining husbandmen* to look under *a'ternoon farmers*, for instance!

There will undoubtedly be words in this book which readers growing up in the counties surrounding Hertfordshire may claim as their own. Words have never been subject to restriction by county boundaries but what is certain is that those included on the following pages were in use in Hertfordshire both in and before Grey and Carbery's day.

The spelling of any written version of what was a solely oral language is bound to be somewhat arbitrary, but Grey and Carbery managed this difficult task with great success. Sometimes a little imagination is needed, and a few tries at speaking a word out loud may be necessary before it can be tracked down. As Edwin Grey explained in *Cottage Life in a Hertfordshire Village*, 'labourers would never use long words (if they could possibly avoid it), but would always shorten them. Harpenden was always spoken of as "Ard'n", and so on, for as they themselves said, "We don't trouble ter twist our tongs over 'em." The letter H was never sounded; it was practically dropped altogether. "Wot's the good on it? Words are jest as good a'rout," said one old chap to me, meaning that words are just as good without the H as with it.' Hard-pressed teachers attempting to instil 'proper English' into country children would frequently come up against a parent who would complain, 'Why, my gal cum 'ome t'other day, and said teacher 'ad told 'er as 'ow she'd got ter spell taters with a P!'

Above all, what shines through is the very aptness of the language for what it described. You don't really have to be told what a woman *perkin'* in front of a mirror is doing, or that if you're up to your ankles in *slud*, you're standing in thick, foul mud. And it is also probable that what we have gained in education, we have lost in richness of language – just have a look under *chastisement* at how many ways there were to threaten someone with violence! Our Hertfordshire ancestors may not have had much book larnin' but their language was full of vivid imagery and vigour. As you turn the pages you can, if you listen carefully, hear the olduns talking.

As Grey and Carbery remind us: 'We do well to be proud of our words, to use them, to keep them alive as they deserve'.

Margaret Ward

Acknowledgements and Sources

For the first edition of *Hertfordshire Heritage*, acknowledgements were made to: H. C. Andrews, Hertford; F. G. Gurney, Egginton; Arthur MacDonald, Tring; Archibald Jackson, Sawbridgeworth; Reginald Hine, Hitchin; P. Ilott, Bengeo; R. Webb, Berkhamsted; P. Birchnell, Berkhamsted; Mr Botwright, Abbots Langley; Mrs George, Oxhey; Miss Sophia King, Glaston; Mr Plested, Watford; and Miss Rose Sale, Hinxworth.

For this revised edition, thanks are also due to Mrs Amy Coburn of Harpenden, a respected local historian who was kind enough to offer her collection of over 90 additional words and phrases.

The principal sources of quotes used by Edwin Grey and Mary Carbery to illustrate particular words or sayings include the works of Geoffrey Chaucer (*c.*1345–1400), Edmund Spenser (1552–1599) and William Shakespeare (1564–1616); the early English bible translations of John Wycliffe (*c.*1329–1384), William Tyndale (*d.*1536) and Miles Coverdale (1488–1568); John Bunyan's *The Pilgrim's Progress* (1678); the agricultural writings of Thomas Tusser (*c.*1520–1580) and William Ellis, an 18th-century Hertfordshire writer, and Reginal Hine's *History of Hitchin* (1927) and *Hitchin Worthies* (1932). There are many references to the *Hertfordshire Sessions Rolls*, which have been published in ten volumes (1905–1957) covering the period 1589–1843.

What do our words tell us?

We learn from our words their history, lineage, place of origin, the changes they have gone through, and their meaning, or the meaning we have come to attach to them.

They tell us besides, something of the outlook and characteristics of the folk we were and in the main still are: God-fearing, kind, honest, trustworthy, shrewd, tenacious. They show our boundless love for Our Country, for the good earth, and for those who serve the land, both man and beast, at whose side many of us toil for our daily bread.

There are many words for those features which make our Hertfordshire so lovely and so dear: uplands and dales, woods, streams, deep winding lanes, ancient roads and tracks and ways.

What more can we learn about ourselves?

That we are a brave bold folk as history witnesses. There is no dialect word for the Latin surrender and submission. Our foes knuckle under to us. And we have between forty and fifty words for our ways of showing them who is master!

In spite of our warlike spirit, we are very gentle with children: our little atomies, chicks, shrimps, brats, images and morsels. The least-un (youngest) is our honey, our poppet, our lil mouse. Older boys are yong warmints, pickles, turks and, if extra mischievous, gallus yong faggits.

Kindly, too, we have ever been towards our neighbours, ready to share a trouble, to lend a hand. A man would not hesitate to rate his wife if she had been 'blatin' 'bout the neebours,' or 'ferretin' into other folks' consarns.'

In days gone by, a man's 'missus' had to be home-keepin', becomin' (well-behaved), quiet-spoken, trim and tidy in appearance, handy with her needle, able to cure and pickle the baconer, to bake bread and to turn out our favourite Hertfordshire dishes: swimmers, fatty, lardy and crinklin' cakes, faggits, pumpkin pie, figgy-duff, black pudd'n, onion dumplins, pigs-fry, etc. She had to be able to fry a mouse to cure the whooping-cough, to make yarb (herb) tea, and dunny-leaf 'bacca, groundsel poultices, marshmallow ointments, cowslip, dandelion and ginger wines. At times she might be called on to bring up a 'arry-pig, or a cosset lamb.

In spite of her many duties, the missus must on no account become a drodge: she must manage her work and not let it get on top of her.

First and foremost she must turn the children out beautiful (clean and tidy) and keep an ever watchful eye on her young daughter. Perty (pretty) as a pictur' very like, but handsome is as handsome does. A country gal oughter look healthy, with red cheeks and bright eyes, an' fer that she mun (must) eat up her wittles an' not goo pimblin' her meat (food) like a yallerfaced pimmick … She mun dress neat an' sootable an' mind her manners, and niver goo gaddin' with flighty moggies or hob-a-nob with sockly draggle-tail pieces (slummocks, mawks, rattles) an' sich as them. Mother mun see as her gal don't never git talkin' to any o' they idle scroungers as won't do a honest day's work or turn a hand for no one. Even a harmless chap what's a button-short, is bes' kep' at a distance. A gal nacherly don't know a cus, douse or twister be (by) the look o' him … she can't know, without (unless) her mother tells her, when a chap's off'n his nut, ner what a mort o' cracky, cranky, onsensible noddies there be in the world: out'n out bedlams and loonies (mugs, gulls, softy-sawnies, joult-skulls) …

The girl's father might know even more words for distracted persons, although he would not use more than one or two at a time. That there should be so many is due to our Hertfordshire way of sizing up the folk we come across and putting each one in his proper class.

We are said by our admirers to have reticence and a habit of understatement: we certainly go our own way, avoiding notoriety, with no wish to be cracked up. We do not crake on about ourselves or our possessions: if, for example, a neighbour comments on our laden trees, we grudgingly admit 'ther med (might) be a tidy few apples'.

On the other hand should anyone dare to disparage Our Country or criticise Hertfordshire weather, at once we are up on our hind legs.

'A lot of rain you seem to get over this way,' you may say, coming yourself from the sheers (shires) and being in consequence a *furiner*.

'Rain! Call this rain?' we snort. 'Weather's a bit dabbly mebbe (or drizzly, smirry, tachy, casalty, etc.).'

On the other hand, real rain which cannot be denied, we call 'a fine teemin' downpour, jest what's wanted,' or 'a good drenchin' pelt as'll make the grass grow'.

Your 'beastly east wind' we call 'a bit of a stinger what'll dry the land fer sowin' the barley.' Perhaps we hum the old song:

> Sow your wheat in sluddy weather,
> In the dust your barley sow.

after which you will hardly call us unmusical. Unmusical, indeed! Have you never heard *We're all jolly fellows who follow the plough* or *The Spotted Cow* or *As I sat on a sunny bank*?

Furiners who think they know us, though not so well may be as we know them, say we are a level-headed folk without imagination or sense of beauty – though we admire a cherry tree in bloom as much as anyone, or the wind running over a field of corn. They call us unemotional. Well, we are none the worse for that. We know how to hide our feelings. We face facts. We aren't turned from our opinions, either, nor hindered in our work by speechifyers, agitators, ranters, nor by any other sort of Cheap Jack. They think us stupid because we are by nature quiet, contented folk, not for ever wanting to roam away from home. We learnt from our old people that the way to be happy is to enjoy the little things of life and in Our Country they are ever to be found close at hand.

Perhaps I am making ourselves out too perfect? We have had our black sheep. Foolish chaps who sooner or later got nabbed (or nobbled) and shut in the cage or the lock-up, and later found themselves in the County Gaol, where they had to pay fourpence a day for their keep. A bit earlier on they would have been transported or hanged. Sometimes they stayed away from church and went to religious meetings held perhaps in a barn, or 'sold drink on a Sunday to a multitude of people rastling (wrestling) and football playing'. Or they 'harboured vagrants,' or stole a sheep, or held up the Hertford mail. They occasionally stole a horse, or even a fighting-cock from Lord Salisbury's cock-walk. Sometimes they went a-porching (poaching) and traced hares with greyhounds in the snow. Now and again a witch, male or female, was had up for casting spells. All these and more are to be found recorded in Hertfordshire's archives.

Of all the occupations, the most lasting contentment was found and may be found again in the service of the Land. Perhaps the secret of this is that a man can love the Land: to the old-time husbandman, country-bred and born, the Land was of supreme importance, and in his eyes, a creature of almost human intelligence: 'It's foo-ur year sen (since) thisyer field had a dressin', an' it aint forgot it'. Let us hope that the sheen (machine) will not tear away all traces of our old days and old ways.

We, who are Hertfordshire-born, know better than to laugh at the way our people and particularly the old folk talk. We know that dialect is the older and purer form of speech and worthy of respect. Moreover when we hear wook for woke and waked, afeard or frit for afraid, casted for cast, mun, med or mout for must and might, meece for mice, wapses-neestes for wasps'-nests, goo for go, deef for deaf, squi-er and fi-er for squire and fire, we know very well that we are listening to English of the time of Edward III, of the Canterbury Pilgrims, of Chaucer himself.

'Well, I'll niver talk no different,' says Grandfather, 'not for nobody I woon't,' and old Chaucer echoes, 'I thought not to ax of him nothing'. Nor shall we: let Grandfather use as many negatives as he pleases. Shakespeare said, 'I will not budge for no man's pleasure'. In his company the old folk go farther: they drar more closer to the fier, agreeing that they 'niver knowed a more colder Febe[wary ner, come to that, a frost...'

'More sharper,' murmurs Master Shakespeare, 'more sharper than your swords.' (*Henry V*)

There are many more of our words which belong to Elizabethan days and earlier: dar for dare, frorn for frozen, brickle for brittle, clean for entirely, crake for boast, commonly for usually, besides drouthy, flaggy, gobbet, huggermugger, scruse. Edmund Spenser used them all, and he 'laboured to restore to their place as to their rightful heritage, such good and natural English words as have been long time out of use and almost clean disinherited' (Thomas Warton).

This must surely have meant out of use by people of fashion, for country folk were using them all the time with every intention of holding them fast. Among country folk were reckoned justices, parsons who preached in dialect and squires who from time to time went to the Court to pay their respects to the Queen. It was then that Edmund Spenser might have noticed the behaviour of certain 'unseasoned courtiers' among the new rich who, fearing to be taken for the country bumpkins they despised, scorned to use dialect words, *'those terrible marks of the beast to the truly genteel'* (Thomas Hardy) ... so they tittered and nudged one another when our squires gave the Queen the news of Hertfordshire in their everyday speech and Elizabeth, we may be sure, responded vigorously in the dialect she had learnt in childhood when Our Country was her refuge and first home.

From this time, in spite of the Queen's favour and Spenser's efforts, the use of dialect declined among those who had 'book-learning'. Perhaps the Stuarts discouraged it: it may have been too difficult for them, as vexatious as the deep furrows made by our big ploughs, into which poor Prince Charles was apt to tumble when hunting from Theobalds or Royston.

Kings and courtiers, however, whether Tudor, Stuart or Hanoverian, made no odds to us country folk. When parson and squire fell away – except when talking down to us – we stood by our old cry (our manner of speech), all the more when in time we began to get about the county and found to our surprise that there are three versions of the dialect. A man from Tring, we discovered, spoke differently from one of Ware, and a Dunstable or St Albans man unlike either; even when they were using the same words they pronounced them differently. One thing they had (and we have) in common, the lilt and intonation which are unmistakable in all true Hertfordshire folk. It has been said against us that we drawl and make two syllables out of one, but a sensitive ear hears, not two syllables, but the modulation from one musical sound to another: *good marnin'*, for example, would be given four if not five separate tones: many expressions of surprise, anger, even of love, fall or rise by intervals of thirds, fourth or fifths. This ever varying quality of intonation gives that charm and tunefulness which modern speech and particularly the cockney dialect are said to lack.

We cannot, unfortunately, praise the wayward pronunciation of dialect words and vowels by our folk. Take for example, the sound *oo* as in rule, true, do, too, etc., as if it had a very short *i* or *e* before it (as in *it* and *egg*). It may be true that we sounded *oo* that way in Saxon days, and true that Chaucer wrote and presumably said riule (riool) for rule and triuth (triooth) for truth just as we do (the words *do* and *too*, pronounced by us as *dioo* and *tioo*, are sometimes written *dew* and *tew*, but that does not represent the sound). It is none the less an uncouth sound. Uglier still is our *ea*, *ee*, a sound which only a native can produce, something like the French *eu* (as in *peu*) instantly followed by *e*. Ugly too our caow for cow!

In some districts we put *i* before *a*, rian for rain, siame for same. The name of the only English pope, a Hertfordshire man, was sometimes written Brykespeare. Like Chaucer and Wycliffe we preferred *oo* to *o*. We changed our coot when we got hoom. We milked the nanny-goots and strooked (stroked) th' lil kids, 'a-pooking ther nooses inter th' pial.' In other places we turn *i* into *oi*: 'Moy oi! What a proice!' and *oi* into *i*: 'Sukey's bi'lin', missus, coom an' miake th' teue (tea).'

It is true that we think nothing of clipping letters from our words, *h* in front and *g* behind and *d*, *t*, *r*, even whole syllables when we think fit, such as the *ly* of adverbs, but we add letters here and there in return, as in chimbley-cornder, townd or scrush.

These changes seem inconsistent until one remembers that we country folk were speaking English by ear for a thousand years before we learnt to read and write and so to see our mistakes. In that time *scholards* stole a march on us and wrote their way of talking in books as being the proper fashion, when 'very like our cry was properer still', or so we thought.

Edwin Grey
Mary Carbery
1948

A

a. a, an: 'A apple tree in a archard.'

a². before numerals and nouns of quantity: A two-three, a'arf a pint, a many, a plenty, a goodish few.

a³. before participles: a-huntin', a-fishin'; 'sweet flowers a-growin' and a-blowin'.'

a⁴. he: 'A (he) babbled on green fields.' (Shakespeare, *Henry IV.*)

a⁵. have, has, had: 'Ye could a ast me.'

a⁶. at: 'I seed a fox roun' th' 'en-'us a brekfas' time.'

a⁷. of: 'a-coo-urse', of course.

a⁸. on: 'The gate's a t'other side o' th' road.' 'See yer a Chuesday (Tuesday)'; ''im as (who) can't ride a 'oss-back mun (must) goo a-foot'; 'Chimbley's afire!'

a⁹. in, in the: 'Time ye was a-bed'; 'Postman calls twicet a day.'

a¹⁰. with: 'Coom along a me, me daer'; 'It poo-ured a rain.'

a¹¹. half: 'Gooin' on fer 'a' pas' ten.'

Park Street, Hatfield c.1900 when it was a busy shopping area, just the right place to meet friends and neighbours: 'Glad to see ye about again.'

a-be. to let alone: 'You jist let 'er a-be'; 'Leave me a-be.'

abear, abide. endure: 'I can't abear the sight of a cat.' 'An' *I* can't abide meece; I 'ould liefer (rather) ev a cat.'

about. doing: 'What be you about in my gardin?' 2 happening: 'What's about in the kitchen?' 3 out, recovered: 'Glad to see ye about again.'

above a bit. a good deal.

abundance. a great deal: 'It had snowed abundance that night; it lay very deep and I had no stockin's on so the snow got into my shoes.' (Hine, *Hitchin Worthies*)

accorder, corder. according to: 'Corder ter what I 'ears,' is a common ending to a sentence.

account, count. worth: ''E eent o'much 'count.'

ackle. work, do: 'I'll ackle it!'

acrost, crost. across.

ad, a', ed. has, had. **ant,** has not, had not: 'Th' po'r chap 'ant niver 'ad no chanst.'

addle. to confuse. 'A o'd (old) addle-'ade': a muddle-headed old person.

a done now. have done, stop it.

afeard. afraid: 'Fie, my lord, fie! A soldier and afeard.' (Shakespeare, *Macbeth*)

afore. before: 'Will you go on afore?'

ag. bramble or any prickly bush. 2 a valley with a sharp bend in it.

agin, agen. again. 2 against, near to: 'Th' rake's agin th' 'ay-rick.' 3 in anticipation of: 'Agin a rainy day.'

agog. eager and ready.

ah. yes, and according to intonation, ah expresses assent, astonishment, enquiry, suspicion, admiration; it may mean: 'What did I tell you, 'e caught you proper!' or 'Now you know!'

ail. to be ill: ''Er dunt ail nothin', not now.'

ails, awns, yawns, hails, hulls. husks of corn, beard of barley.

aim. to intend.

aint, baint, aren't, een't. am not, are not, is not, has not, have not: 'Aint ye p'oot-nigh (pretty near) done?' 'No, I aren't.' 'Aint ye got a saw?' 'I aint got ne'r a saw.' 'Aint yer boy anywheers about t' lend a 'and?' 'No 'e *een't.* An' pray aint you got nowt ter do but ax a lot o' silly questions? Taint your consarn.'

ak, akky. hark, hark ye.

akker. acre, a field, arable land. 2 a measurement of surface, 150 sq. rods or perches or 4840 sq. yds.

al'ays, ol'as. always.

all as is, all as one. 'It seems 'tis all as one an' no use what ye do or don't do.'

all manners o'. all sorts.

all o' a sort. alike.

all 'olland, all 'ollan'tide. All Hallow tide, All Saints.

along-a, all along-a, along 'uth. with: ''owd Starlin's brung 'is tools: 'e's startin' along-a us t'morrer.' 2 owing to: 'It's all along-a you as I lost my place.'

am. also **be.** am, are: 'I are a-gooin'.' 'Be you gooin'?' Am is used before the prefix *a*. If be is used the *a* is dropped.

an', 'n'. and: 'You'n me an' the baby.'

an' all. indeed: 'Ye can't do't, I tell 'e.' 'Can't I an' all! Ye'll see.' 2 that sort of thing: 'Lest the other (swine) turne again and all to rent [rend] you.' (*Coverdale's Bible*)

anigh. near: 'Doon't yer niver coom a-nigh my 'ouse n'moer' (no more).

an'inted. wicked: 'An an'inted young rascal.'

anough, enow. enough: 'Anough t'git th' better on yer' (more than one can bear).

answer. reason: 'See 'ere, yoong, chap, ye're 'alf a 'ou-er late this marnin ... overdone it (overslept), ev'e? Master'll want a better answer ner thaat.' 2 to retaliate: ''E sez that o' me, do 'e? I'll soon answer 'im.' 3 to be impertinent: 'I woun't (will not) ev yer answerin' me ser saacy.' 4 to succeed: ''E'll find out t'wunt answer.' 5 to back, be surety for another: 'I'll answer for yer, no fear.'

ant. see **ad.**

antics. silly behaviour, pranks.

any'ow meal. a make-shift meal.

any road. in any case.

anywheers. anywhere.

Aperl. April: 'When Aperl blows his horn, 'tis good for hay and corn.' (Country saying.)

apern. apron.

apern-string-'old. property held in virtue of a wife.

apple, also **bottle.** to form tubers or bulbs: 'Me taters be n't applin' like they ed ough'ter.'

aps. aspen.

apt. inclined.

ara, ary, arra. e'er a, any.

arbury, oldbury. (several variations), ancient forts.

archard, oorchard. garden, orchard.

are, I're. am, I am.

a'ready. already.

argify. to argue.

argimint. argument.

arout. without.

'arry-pig, anthony-pig. runt or weakling. See also **dillon**.

arse up'ards. awkward way of doing a job.

art. calling: 'The art, mystery or handicraft of a clock-maker.' (Herts Sessions Rolls)

arth, yarth. earth. **arth'n.** earthen.

arwig, yarwig, arrywig, errywig. earwig.

as. who, that, which: 'That noo mare as master's tuk a fancy fer, be n't sound.' 'The vet as coom t' see o'd powny, reckernised the mare threcly (directly) 'e clapped eyes on 'er.'

as ever was. redundant words: 'Las' Sunday as ever was.'

as th' sayin' is. a favourite and usually irrelevant expression used at the end of a sentence: 'Sometimes I don't touch beer for weeks together, as the sayin' is.'

ast, also **ax.** to ask: 'Ast Tom,' says master, so I axed Tom.' 'A certayne man found him (Joseph) wandrynge out of his waye in the feld and axed him what he soughte.' (Tyndale's *Pentateuch*) 'And for my werke nothing will I ax.' (Chaucer)

at. to: 'He came at the Slough of Despond.' 'He went up and I followed till we came at a golden gate.' (*Pilgrim's Progress*) 2 from: 'Seke helpe at him.' (*Coverdale's Bible*)

a'ter. after: 'And atyre this his modir (mother) did arise, And lyfte him up softly into the stall.' (Lydgate)

a'termath, a'tergrass, a'termead. also **lattermath, eft crop, tail crop, rowen, hucker-me-buck.** second crop of grass.

a'ternoon farmers. also **declining husbandmen,** farmers who are not prospering.

athirt. athwart, across. See also **over-thirtin'**.

atoms, atomies. children, small creatures.

atomy, anatomy. skeleton: 'He's wore away to a atomy!' 'Thou atomy, thou!' (Shakespeare, 2 *Henry IV*)

atween, atwixt. between: 'Let it be a secret atwixt the two on us.'

av akker. see **shot**.

awk'ard, ock'ard. awkward, difficult.

awns. see **ails**.

ax. see **ast**.

aye. yes, in answer to a direct question.

aye? aye-what? What did you say?

B

'bacca. tobacco.

back. to wager, warrant.

back a hedge. to allow short thorn to grow up on one or other side of a hedge as protection for the quick, and called inside or outside back according to position.

back answer. impertinent retort.

back of. behind.

back'us. outhouse.

backway. backyard of house: 'round the backway'.

baconer. a pig fattened for curing.

bad. ill: ''e took bad wery sooden.' **badly,** poorly, ill.

badger, bodger. dealer, see also **higgler.** 2 rascal: 'artful badger'. **'oss bodger.** horse dealer.

badger-legged, also **bandy-legged.** bow-legged: ''e's that badger-legged, 'e c'ld stop a pig in a twitchel.'

bag. sack. **bag-up,** to put into sacks.

baggin'. see **fag.**

bait. a halt. 2 rest and feed for man and horse: 'The sun ... At night doth bait his steeds.' (Spenser) 3 to pasture sheep.

bake and **cake.** condition of soil after heavy rain.

balk, baulk. a ridge between two furrows. **balk and burril,** ridge and furrow. 2 a division between fields about 2ft. high made of earth:
> 'There horse being tied on a balk,
> Is ready with thief for to walk.' (Tusser)

3 cart-baulk, a cart-track inside a field usually next the hedge, see **headland.** 4 to overlook and miss ploughing a portion of land. 5 to refuse food: ''e balks 'is meat' (food). Balks, once 'the stronghold of wild flowers,' were levelled and ploughed over after the Enclosure Acts were passed.

ballyraggin'. continuous teasing.

bams, also **tiddlers.** sticklebacks. **bammin',** fishing for tiddlers.

bandy. a club: 'When the field is cleared of ant-heaps, we ... beat the mould about with bandies.' (Ellis)

bang. right, abruptly: 'Best goo bang away.'

banger. anything very large of its kind. 2 knock, fall, collision. 3 a flagrant lie, an unbelievable story.

bangle. to knock about. 2 to hang loosely: 'His hat bangled over his head.'

bangled up with slud. covered with mud.

bangy. muddy.

bank. to break up ant-hills (ant-banks) with bandies.

bar, bargh. a bridle way up a hill.

barge. to force a way: ''e coom baargein' in loike a bull at a gate.'

bark. to graze.

barmy. silly: 'As barmy as lights.' (Herts saying.)

barning. barn buildings. 2 bays in a barn: 'Bays o' barnin' full o' turnups.'

barntasker. threshing man. His task was to thresh and clean 25 bushels a week. See also **thrailer.**

barrer. wheelbarrow.

bash. to hit: 'Goo in an' bash 'em':
'A woman, a whelp and a walnut tree,
The better ye bash 'em, the better they be.' (Old saying.)

bashin'. a beating. 2 exceedingly: 'A bashin' wet time.'

bassan or **bast-rope.** rope of twisted fibre: 'They stake their horses with bassan- (basten) ropes.'

baster. a blow.

bastin'. a thrashing.

bat. a hit: ''e fotch me a bat in me faace.'

bat-folding, bat-fowling. sparrow-catching after dark in winter with nets on long poles, drawn along walls and hedges.

bauldrick. horse-hide thong by which the clapper was fastened to a church bell, renewed and re-hung by the village smith when required.

bavin. a small bundle of 4ft. sticks, bound with a withy. A bavin tied with 2 withies was a hedger's perquisite. **bavinin',** tying into faggots.

bay. a space in barn or hay-shed between the main beams. A barn consists of a number of bays according to the number of beams.

be, bees. am, is, are: 'Ther it be! Ketch a 'olt (hold) on 't.' See also **am.** 2 by. **be that,** by that time. **be** is not a mispronunciation but a Saxon preposition meaning by.

bear and hang. of a cart, when the load bears on the horse's back or hangs so that the shafts tilt upward.

beat out. to persuade, convince: 'I could not beat him out of it.' (*Pilgrim's Progress*)

beautiful. clean and tidily turned out.

become. to suit: 'Jist look at my noo 'at! I don't become it at all.'

becomin'. well-behaved.

bed'ard. to bed: 'Dint ye ough'ter be gooin' bed'ard?'

bedlam. lunatic: 'Some said they were fools, some they were bedlams, and some they were outlandish men.' (*Pilgrim's Progress*)

beggared. an imprecation: 'I'll be beggared if I'll stand any mo'e o'yer imperance.'

beholden. owing a debt to.

bell-man. crier, originally night-watchman. The town-crier wore a blue coat with silver buttons and carried a bell and a staff.

bells. the Ting-tang or Sermon-bell, the 5-minute bell, rung to announce a sermon.

bellus. to bustle about.

besom. a 'witchy' woman.

best. to get the better of: 'Dint I tell ye as 'e'd best ye? 'E bestes iverybody as 'es dealins w'th 'im.'

bet, also **bested.** beaten: 'I wount be bet be it iver so.'

betel, bedel. a wooden bat or mallet.

better ner or **of.** more than: 'Better ner two mile.' ''Tis anough to git the better on you' (more than one can bear).

betternmost. best.

between-lights. twilight.

bever, baver. a glass of beer in the middle of the morning with or without bread and cheese (see **'lowances**). Old English *beive*, drinking.

bible-backed. round-shouldered, also used for a cow's rounded back.

bide. stay, remain: 'I was born in thisyer 'ouse an' I'll bide 'ere ser long as I live.' 'Let the ladder bide wher 't is.' 'Bide a-long o' me, wunt 'e?' 2 wait: 'Bide 'ere while (till) I come fer yer.'

big, bigness. size, large or small: ''bout as big as a pin's 'ead.'

bile, biol. to boil.

bile the pot. to cook.

bill. billhook: 'Ye din't ough'ter grind but the one side of a bill.'

bin, a-bin. been.

bird-minder. also crow-keeper, crow-scarer, crow-starver, crow-tender, boy who scares rooks at the autumn sowing and sparrows as the corn ripens: 'I be gooin' a-crow-starvin'; where's me clackers?' The clacker or clapper is a flat wooden bat with a hinged flap which makes a loud banging when swung up and down. Crow-scarer's cries: 1 'I'll pick up my clackers, An' knock 'e down back'ards, Ee yow, ee yoo, ee yoo, Cra-ah, cra-ah, cra-ah.' 2 'Hullo! Hullo! an ol' black crow.' (Repeated)

bit. somewhat: 'a bit older'n me.' 2 small, insignificant: 'She aint but a bit o' a gal.' 3 a strange incident, news: 'Pray! that's a bit, ain't it? 'ow did ye coom ter 'ear on't?' 4 food: 'I 'ad a bit as I come along.'

bite. to trick.

black. a smut.

black-'oss. large black ant: 'Them's black-oss-pissum's eggs' (ant larvae).

blam! blam it. a mild expletive.

blandigo, blendigo. showery, cloudy.

blasphemious. unseemly.

blast. an expletive. 2 a blight: 'Blasted with the east wind.' (Genesis 41. 6.)

blate. to bleat, bellow. 2 gossip: 'Ther ye goo! A-blatin' 'bout yer neebours!'

blave, bleeve. to believe.

blew. spent: 'blew all his money'.

blight. an unkind condition of atmosphere said to blight young crops, producing blast, blight and strokes of wheat.

blink. a very small light or fire: 'Ther weren't not a blink o' light.' 'Ther's jist a blink o' fire: ye med blow it oop with th' bellers.' 2 twinkle: 'The stars began to blink.'

blinkerd. a blind person.

blizzy. an out-door fire. 2 a flaring fire indoors: 'Les (let us) ev a bit of a blizzy.'

blobbers, blubbers, blothers. flatulence, bubbles.

blossom-time. Spring.

blow. an expletive: 'I'll be blowed ef I wull.'

blown. broken: 'Ford bridge is so blown and damaged by the late floods ... the same should be rebuilt.' (Herts Sessions Rolls, 1773)

blub. to cry.

blubbered. tear-stained, swollen from crying.

bobbish. well in health, lively.

bode, bord. to foretell.

bodged-up, botched-up. work done roughly.

bodgel. to bundle up anyhow. 2 garments bunched or rucked up.

bodger. see **badger.**

body linen. underclothes.

boffle, buffle. to confuse: 'I wer reg'lar boffled.'

boggard, bogget, bogle. scarecrow: 'I seed a tattered bogget an that's all as I see.' See **scarecrow.**

bomble. bumble bee. Also **humble.**

bomby, bumpy. a low marshy place. 2 a sodden dung-yard.

bone in my leg. excuse for doing nothing.

bone lazy. idle, a waster.

boost up. to hitch a load on the back by a movement of the shoulders.

borrer. to borrow: 'e'd borrer the norse (nose) off'n yer face ef ye'd let 'im.' **borrerin,'** borrowing.

bottle. a bundle of hay or grass tied up for fodder. 2 a small barrel or keg carried by haymakers. See also **apple.**

bottom. low ground, often marshy. **no bottom,** unreliable boggy land.

bouge. bulge.

The delivery cart about to go out on the rounds from the village shop at Shenley:
'Boughten bread be n't a patch on 'ome-made.'

boughten. bought: 'Boughten bread be n't a patch on 'ome-made.'

bourn. a stream. 2 a boundary, often a deep wide ditch.

bout. to plough into bouts. The plough by working forwards then backwards throws two furrows together. Each ridge has two bouts. Bouts are also called wheat-stitches.

box o'whustles. contemptuous name for the church-organ: 'A pious box o'whustles what nob'dy wanted.' The organ was greatly resented when it superseded the village church-orchestra: the great fiddle (double-bass), grandfather fiddle (cello), 2 or 3 little fiddles, flute, clarinet and bassoon.

branch. stream.

brat. child (naughty).

bread an' pull it. a slice of dry bread.

breath. words, language.

breathe. to let out a secret: 'Doont yer breathe it to no one. Niver a breath on't's got out 'bout ere.'

breeders, luck breeders. boys retained by players in a game of marbles, supposed to bring luck.

breeding-stone. see **plum-pudding stone**, conglomerate.

bren-chase. bread and cheese. 2 the name given by children to hawthorn leaves, dog-rose shoots, and to the seed pod of the mallow (maller-chase), all of which were taken with bread.

bren-seam. bread and lard or dripping.

brestfust, brakfus'. breakfast.

brickle. brittle.

broke, bruk. broken.

broom. a birch-broom: 'Furiners calls 'em besoms, but we calls 'em brooms.'

browse-wood. bushy wood, due to cattle browsing on the shoots. 2 the bushy head of an oak.

budge. to move: 'You budge out o' 'ere ...'

bug, bugaboo. bogey.

bulk. shop counter.

bull-rush. to rush about: 'Ther ye goo, a-bull-rooshin' all o-er the place.'

bullymong. a mixture of green fodder.

bumble. to hum.

bu'n, burn. **bu'nt, brunt,** burnt.

Outside the Green Man at Ickleford. Cars travelled too fast for some: 'Ther' ye goo, a-bull-rooshin' all o'er the place.'

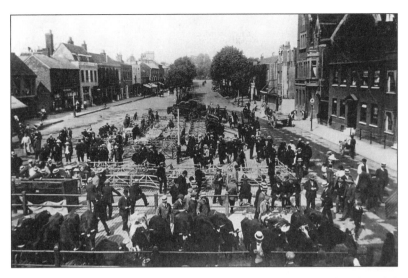

The weekly cattle market outside the Town Hall, St Albans: 'Farmer did ough'ter shift that ther buntin' cow.'

bundle off. to leave hurriedly.

bunt. a shove: 'Ere, gi' me a bunt oop.' 2 to butt: 'Farmer did ough'ter shift (move away) that ther buntin' cow.'

burril. furrow. See **balk.**

bust, busted. burst.

butt. end, extremity. 2 larger end of a felled tree, also called **arse-eend**: 'Ye mun (must) load timber butt for'ost' (foremost). 3 projections in the corners of fields, left untilled during ploughing, but eventually cultivated, if not with the same crop, with potatoes, etc.

button-short. not quite 'all there': 'Po'r chap, 'e's a button-short an' no good t' nobody.'

by. to pass by: 'Postman'll be by any minute.' 2 from: 'I 'eard it by me neebour.'

bymby. by and by.

C

caddle. disorder.

caddy. van boy, errand boy.

cadge. to live on another. 2 to beg in an indirect way: 'Can I cadge a match off'n you?'

cadger. a huckster. 2 one who gets a living by questionable means, or who borrows without intention of repaying.

cage. also **lock-up**, a house or room in a village where a disorderly person could be detained.

cagmag. coarse tough food. 2 disorder (caddle).

cake. condition of soil, see also **bake**.

caleb jay. a figure of fun, overdressed or in rags, said to be from the French, *qu'el objet*.

call. need, occasion: 'Ther aint no call fer us to meddle, t'aint none of our business.'

caller. pale and sickly: ''e looks proper caller.'

callerboshes. unfledged nestlings: 'Leave them nestes a-be. If ye take them callerboshes they'll on'y die.'

call over the coals. tell off.

canker, canker-bloom. wild rose.

cankers. sore places in the mouth; usually of children who put metal (coins) in their mouths.

carlick. charlock (wild mustard). 2 to weed charlock from corn: 'We're got a job a-carlicking.'

carlickers. boys employed to weed.

carp. to find fault.

carrier. see **higgler**.

carry. to behave: 'He carried it wonderful loving to him.' (*Pilgrim's Progress*)

cart-hovel. cart shed.

casalty. casualty, precarious, uncertain: 'Marnin', Jarge. Casalty weather, ben't it?' 2 feeble: ''er's old an' casalty.' 3 animals which have died a natural death: 'They gyppoes (gypsies) eats casalties.'

catch, also **ketch.** catch.

cattern. St Catherine, patron saint of lace-makers. **keeping cattern,** an old custom among lace-makers living in W. Herts of having family parties on the Saint's day, November 25th. Cattern cakes were eaten on this occasion.

'cause, 'cos. because. **cause why,** the reason: 'I dint clean out th' 'en'us (hen-house). Cause why? Cos it waant (was not) my work.'

cawin. woolgathering, daydreaming.

centre down. settle down.

chaffer. to bargain, to bandy words.

cha-ir, cheer. chair.

champion. great, well done. 2 open country (champaign): 'The champion with its lynches and balks.' (Herts Sessions Rolls)

chank. persistent impudence: 'See 'ere! Ef ye let me ev any moe o'yer chank, I'll cut ye a-two.'

chank over. talk over, chew over.

chapman. an itinerant trader.

chaps. commonly used for men.

charivari. a noisy derisive serenade.

charms. see **cures.**

chase, chaser. hunter: 'Thou may lick (like) to keep a chase.'

chastisement. 'I'll cha-ahstise 'im, bash 'im, baste 'im, brain 'im, thwack 'im, punish 'im; fetch 'im a bat on 'is face, a box on his (y)ear, a crap, a clout, a crack on 'is 'ead, a cuff, a cut, a dob, a sock. I'll cop 'im one, give 'im beans, punch 'is 'ead, cotch 'im a sliver, cow 'im down, goo fer 'im, 'ev a smack at 'im, lay into 'im, make 'im sit up, make 'im smart, floor 'im, fetch 'im a swiper, fetch 'im a stinger, let 'im ev it, properly dress 'im, tan 'is 'ide, lamm inter 'im, quamp 'im, warm 'im, whop 'im. I'll giv 'im a bastin', a drubbin', a hidin', a jacketin', a larrupin', a leatherin', a lickin', a socketer, a tannin', a throshin', a trouncin', a whackin', a wallopin'. I'll giv 'im what fer, I'll make 'im 'oller, I'll make 'im laugh a tother side of his face, I'll give 'im pen and ink, what 'e ast (asked) fer, what 'e desarves an what 'e'll niver fergit. I'll larn 'im proper. I'll cut 'im a-two.'

chaw. to chew. 2 to nag (jaw): ''e kep' on a-chawin' 'bout it.'

check, cheek. to mock: 'They that were crucified with him, checked him also.' (Tyndale, *New Testament*)

cherm, charm. noise of children, chorus of birds. 2 to charm bees, to repeat a sound until the swarm settles.

chibble, chimble. to nibble.

chibblin'. flaking of plaster on a wall.

chick. a young child. 2 'One o' the white 'en's chicks,' a common description of anyone rather ostentatiously good.

childern. children.

chimbley, chimley. chimney. **chimbley-cornder,** chimney corner.

chine. to cut chops through.

chinkle. chink, tinkle.

chiny. china.

chip in. to taunt, interrupt. 2 to come unasked.

chippin' an' choppin'. continually changing.

chirpy. in good spirits.

chit. a child or young person: 'chit of a girl'. 2 to sprout: 'I have known barley chit in 7 hours.' (Mortimer)

chitterlings. edible part of pig's intestines.

chivvy. to chase.

choose. to wish: 'Yer father dunt choose ye should goo t' the fa-ir w'thout (unless) I goo along w'th 'e.'

choosed. chose.

chop. to scold: 'You bet master dint 'arf chop at me.' 2 to barter.

christmas. evergreens and holly used for Christmas decoration. This custom originated with the Druids: 'Where Druidism prevailed the houses (such as they were) were decked with evergreens in December, so that the sylvan spirits might repair to them and remain un-nipped with frost and cold winds until a milder season had renewed the foliage of their darling abodes.' (Chandler, *Travels in Greece*)

chu'ch. church: 'Ye're not goin' t' chu'ch in that dutty shut?' (dirty shirt). Hinxworth.

chuck. to throw a short distance: 'Chuck us (to me) th' 'ammer.'

chuesday. Tuesday.

chuff, shuff. shy, surly.

chump, chunk. block or log of wood: 'Firewood for sale in chumps or bundles.'

chunterin'. mumbling.

churry. cherry.

claa. to claw, clutch hurriedly: 'Cla-a 'olt o' th' rope ...' 2 to scramble: 'Ye should 'a seed ol' Tom, a-claain' oop the wa'nut tree when farmer's bull come fer im.'

claain' an' bellusin'. bustling about.

clack. idle chatter, over-talkative.

clacker. clapper, see **bird-minder**.

claggy. matted hair in children or pets. 2 muddy (Claggy Bottom, Kimpton).

clamber. to climb. 2 to clamour: 'The village is clamberin' fer o'd passon (parson) t' coom back.'

clap. to shut: 'Clap the gate to a'ter them cows.' 2 to put on quickly: 'He but just stirred his hat and clapped it on again, sitting on his tayle, and replied to the Justice he would go home when he had made an end of his drink.' (Herts Sessions Rolls, 1686) 3 to knock: ''e come clappin' on the door fit t' wake the dead.' ''e done (did) the same to me, a-clapitin' on the door a'ter we was all abed.'

clap eyes on. to see.

clap-gate. see **kissing-gate**.

clap up. to make hurriedly, knock up: 'I aint got much of a 'en 'us. I jist clapped it up atween times.'

claps. clasp.

clapses. a contrivance for holding a cow's head still while she is milked. It consists of 2 upright bars, one hinged to allow the cow's head to go through a wooden catch to hold the bars in position behind her horns.

clarrin. a loud shrill noise as of a trumpet (clary).

clarrin an' tearin. a hubbub, rushing noisily about.

clatter. to clank, rattle, talk fast.

clean. entirely: 'It 'ad clean gone out o' me 'ead.'

clean an' 'ansome. satisfactorily.

clean an' simple. easy: 'It aint ser clean an' simple as all that.'

cleave. to split.

clent. cleaned.

clickety-clack. the sound made by pattens: 'I can tell 'e I were thankful when I 'eard 'er patterns coom clickety-clack on the pitchins (cobble stones)'.

clinkin'. tinkling. 2 excellent: 'Twer a clinkin' fine bit o' work.'

clod'opper. a heavy-footed man; wearing big boots.

clog. a wooden-soled shoe. 2 a log tied to an animal's leg to prevent it from straying. 3 an encumbrance: 'I propose never to have a clog to my soul.' (*Pilgrim's Progress*)

clomb, clumb. climbed.

clomp. to stump, as in sense of heavy-booted.

close. secret: 'They kept it close and told no man.' (*New Testament*)

clost. close. **closter,** closer.

clost-go. a narrow escape.

clout. a blow. 2 cloth. 3 small pieces of rag. **clouted shoon,** shoes wrapped in clouts to muffle the tread: 'And put my clouted brogues from off my feet.' (Shakespeare, *Cymbeline*)

clump, clumpetin'. to walk noisily.

cobble. to sew badly.

codger. a testy old man, 'artful old codger'.

coil. turmoil.

collar. seize, steal. 2 take in hand, train to work.

collywest. awry, in the wrong direction: 'It's all along o' collywest,' a saying when things go wrong.

come. came. 2 at: 'A year come primrose-time.' 3 to happen, become: 'What's come to ye, me lad? Ye dint ough'ter goo 'bout yer job lookin' like snow in 'arvist! Boock yerself oop an 'ev a bit o' foon (fun)! Yer trouble aint noothin' at all, I lay!'

come down. to fall: 'He come down tiddly bump, come down wallop, 'e did.'

come over. to become: 'I come over fainty-like.' 2 to realise: 'It come o-er me sudden that I aint done honest be master an' I'm gwine t' tell 'im.'

comfable. comfortable.

commonly. usually.

congee. bow: 'He made them a very low congee.' (*Pilgrim's Progress*)

conquer. horsechestnut, tree and nut.

consarn. business: 'other folks' consarns'.

contrary. wilful: 'Contra-iry! Lord love ye! That's 'ow God made females, an' ther's nowt a man can do but put up w'th 'em.'

cooch. a very large box.

cool the heart. to let off steam: 'Cooling their hearts with a murder.' (Hine, *History of Hitchin*)

coot. coat: 'The coot was without seme.' (Coverdale, *New Testament*)

cop. to catch it: 'You'll cop it from master.' 2 to strike: ''e cop me sich a whack.' 3 to make an end: 'It might a copped me off.' 4 to arrest.

copper. policeman.

copses and **ladders.** extensions of a farm cart.

corder. see **accorder**.

core. a small island in a stream. See **island**.

cosset. a lamb brought up by hand. 2 to comfort, cherish.

cotch, cotched, catched. caught.

cotchel, codgel. a small or odd amount; in haymaking, the last of the drags, less than a load. 2 contrive, scrape together.

cotter. a wedge of wood or iron, to fasten door or shutters. 'To cotter the shetters', to open or shut outside shutters from inside the room.

cou'n't. could not.

'count. consider. See also **account**.

counterfeit. to make counterfeit coins: 'Counterfitting, clipping and coining and venting,' making and passing counterfeit money. (Herts Sessions Rolls)

country. county or district. Our Country means Hertfordshire to a Herts man; sometimes his own district.

coupiss. coppice. See **spring**.

cowcumber. cucumber.

cowed. humbled: ''e got a trounchin' as cowed 'im down proper.'

crack. a blow, rap. 2 aperture between hinges: 'I peeked through the cracks of the barne-door.' 3 a moment: 'Wait half a crack.' 4 **crack, crake, crack on,** to boast: ''e do crack on 'bout 'is gardin.' 5 **crack up,** to praise.

cracky. crazy.

cranky. difficult, queer.

crap. a blow.

cribblin', also **kibblin'.** hobbling: 'Po'r ol' Gammy, 'e's cribblin' along, lame as a cat.'

crickets. cricket: 'Did you use to play cricket when you was young, Gran'father? Did you wear flannels like us?' 'Aye, us played crickets an' us played in wer (our) workaday shirts an' trousies an' wer workaday boots, an' some of us ad fancy caps o' red white an' blue w'th tossles (tassels) to 'em, but the more on us 'ad wer billycock-ats.'

crickle. to crumble, break down (of soil). See **ruttle.**

crinklin. crisp.

croffel. to walk with difficulty.

crool. cruel, exceedingly: ''e wus sufferin' somethin' crool, crool bad, 'e wer.'

croons, keroons, also **mazzards, merries.** cherries: 'The best o' cherries is croons an' merries an' 'arfordshere blacks.'

cropped off. cut off by death.

cropper. a fall.

crost. across. See also **acrost.**

crouch. cross. Found in place names, eg Potter's Crouch.

crow. to domineer, triumph over: 'Th' yoong cock crowed a bit too soon: 'e wants 'is comb cuttin'.'

crow-scarer. see **bird-minder.**

crowner's quest. coroner's inquest.

crummy. lousy, poor.

cruppered. checked, sobered: 'That yong chap's growed a bit owdacious, but 'e got a 'idin' fro' school-master an' it's cruppered 'im a bit.'

cry, our cry. dialect. 2 our way of pronouncing words: 'Furiners med (might) say 'arpenden but 'arden's our cry! 'arden, aye, that's ourn.'

The village pond at Harpenden: 'Furiners med say 'arpenden but 'arden's our cry!'

cry off. to leave off.

cry up. to praise.

cub. a wide sweep of road.

cucking-stool. a chair in which scolds and witches were ducked.

cumbered. cluttered, littered.

cunning. wise.

cure. a ridiculous person.

cures and **charms.** For corns: 'Torrify a Slug by the Fire and lay it hot on the Corn.' See **wart.**

cus. an undesirable person.

cuss. curse:

> 'All the months of the year,
> Cuss a fine Februeer.' (Old saying)

cut. a stinging blow.

cut off, cut away. go quickly.

cyart. cart.

D

daater. daughter.

dab, dabbitin. a small quantity: 'a dabbitin lil bit.' 2 a sudden blow. 3 clever, skilful: 'a dab at summin' (arithmetic), a dab hand fer a sick cow.'

dabble. to wash slightly: 'I'll jist dabble me 'ands.' To dip. 2 to paddle in shallow water.

dabbly. showery.

dabby. shabby, flabby.

dabster. quick and artful, a dab hand at something.

dade. did (N.E. Herts): 'What! dade ye, Wool (did you, Will)?' 'Yis, thaat I dade, A-d'ard (Edward).'

da-er. dear.

dag. to thin out plants.

daggin', dagglin'. trailing.

daggins. abundant (crops).

dale. valley.

damp, dampin. drizzle.

dan, randan. wheatings, middlings.

dance. search, chase: ''e led me a fine dance.'

dander. anger, temper.

danderin'. wandering aimlessly.

dane, den, dene. valley, narrow glen, common in place names.

dar, to dare. **darst, darn't, darsent, dassent, dursent,** dare not: 'Ow durst ye? I dassent do sich a thing t' save me life.'

daring. impudent.

dashed. confused, astonished.

daub. clay mixed with straw, chaff and dung, applied in layers on wattled walls. See **wattle.**

dead. absolutely.

decked out. dressed up.

declining husbandmen. see **a'ternoon farmers**.

deef. deaf.

deev'l. the Devil: 'The Deev'l tis!' a common exclamation. It was generally believed that the Devil visited Hertfordshire in various shapes during the reigns of James I and Charles I. He was caught in a cellar at St Albans in the form of a ram, and was killed by a butcher, cut up, sold, and eaten. A pamphlet on the visitations of the Devil was published in 1648.

deev'l-dodger. one who attends both Church and Chapel. 2 artful person.

dene-holes. pits dug by farmers for obtaining chalk. Occasionally used as hiding places. A dene-hole near Dunstable contained charred wood, pottery and bones, thought to be prehistoric.

deny. to refuse: '... denying to take lodgers.' (Herts Sessions Rolls)

desprus. desperate: 'A tarble desprus chap.' 2 great: 'a desprus 'urry.'

dew-beaters, dewsweepers. labourers who come early to work through dewy meadows.

dibbling. putting in plants.

dick, dicky. a low stool. 2 a male donkey.

didder, dodder. to shiver with cold, tremble.

diddicoy. gypsy; untidy person.

differ, differnce. difference.

digged. dug.

dillon, dill, dilling, also **'arry-pig.** the weakling in a litter of pigs.

ding. to impress, bring up: ''e's fer iver dingin' it in my ears.' 2 to throw with violence: ''er dinged the kettle at me.'

ding-dong. uproar of fighting or noise. 2 in good earnest: 'They set to it ding-dong.'

dinking. walking prissily; prinking.

dint, doont, dunt, dunot. does not, did not.

dint ought. should not.

dish. to cheat: 'That chap'll dish yer ef ye don't look out.' 2 to frustrate: 'Master wus upsides with 'im; 'e dished 'is goose proper.'

disible. woman caught when not tidy; in working or untidy clothes.

disrec'lec. to forget.

distempered and **discomposed.** insane. (Herts Sessions Rolls)

dither, see **didder.** to quiver. 2 to menace with quick movements.

dithered. agitated, confused.

ditty. a story.

do. to thrive. 2 to work for: 'She doos fer th' ol' vicar.' 3 to take care of, look after: 'There's not a soul to do for those motherless children.' 4 to bring to a conclusion: (overheard in N.E. Herts – impatient workman to his mate): 'Thaa'll deoo (do)! Tha-er! Thaa'll *deoo*! Tha-er, thaa' *wool* deoo! (*Mate calmly surveying his work*): 'Yes, thaa'll deoo.' 5 to swindle. 6 a festivity. 7 a to-do, fuss. The word do is occasionally spelt dew, approximating to deoo, the common pronunciation: 'The poor peopell dew so hunt mee that I cannot rest from them.' (Hine, *History of Hitchin*: Letter from Edward Lawrence to John Chauncy)

doing-of. doing: 'I were but dooin' o'me dooty.'

do out. to clean.

dob. to put in: 'dob it in'.

doctrine. qualification: 'Ye should goo to a proper doctor, them quacks aint got no doctrine.'

dodman. snail. See **hoddod.**

dollop. a lump.

dolly. a wooden stirrer for the 'wash' in the copper. The dolly's companion was the betty, for straining wet articles over the copper.

done. did: 'I done me best.' 2 settled. 3 cheated.

dook. duke: 'Pray 'oo d'ye think ye are? The Dook o' Stalb'ns?'

doorstep. see **thumb-bit.**

doty, doted. decay in timber, decayed.

double-cunning. acquiring information by unfair means.

doubt. to fear: 'I doubt I'll 'ear she's dade' (dead).

douche, slouche. to throw water over.

dout. to put out: 'Dout the fi-er, me da-er, an' goo ter yer bed.'

down. to cut down: 'It's time we downed th' ol' ook' (oak).

downer. lower: 'Let your end a bit downer.'

downright. at once.

drabbit, rabbit you, also **drat.** confound you.

drabble, draggle. to trail in the mud, to make dirty.

drabble or **draggle-tail,** also **drab.** a woman whose skirt has been trailing in the mud: 'She's a draggle-tail ol' ship (sheep), sure 'nough.'

drad. dreaded: 'What us drad all along 'as 'appened at last.'

drag, drug, drag bat. timber cart. 2 iron shoe used on cart or wagon to retard or stop one wheel and to lessen the weight on the horse. 3 **hand-drag,** a wide wooden rake, hand-hauled behind the cart carrying corn from the harvest field.

drain. any narrow open ditch.

drap. drop.

drar. draw, as in 'drar closer.'

draw. to exhaust, take the goodness from.

dray. to draw: 'The time drayeth near.'

d'rec'ly, threc'ly, d'rec'ly-minute. immediately.

drench. a downpour.

drenchin'. soaking: 'A fine drenchin' rain.'

dress. food for the land: 'Clean land, plenty o'dress, plenty o'labour, then the increase comes.'

dressin'-down. a scolding.

dribble. to pour slowly. 2 to give stingily.

dribblin'. feeble, trifling. 2 a term of contempt: 'A po'r dribblin' piece' (woman).

drodge. an unmethodical woman always at work.

drose, dross. the guttering of a candle.

drove, driv, druv. driven. 2 put to it: 'I wus that druv I dint know what way t' turn fer a penny.'

drownd. to drown: 'Ye mun (must) drownd a two-three o' them kittens.' **drownded,** drowned.

drudge. a servant forced to work long hours by her employer.

drug. dragged.

drumble. sluggish: 'Ther 'e goos, a drumble-'eaded chap, thinkin' o'nowt.'

drunk, lawfully drunk. a man lawfully drunk is intoxicated, but quiet and able to keep on his feet:

'A chap isn't drunk
If he, from the floor
Can get on his legs
And drink one glass the more.'

unlawfully drunk, unable to keep his balance, aggressive and trying 'to kick up a row.' In that state a man is liable to be summoned.

dub. short horns of bull or calf: 'short little dub horns.' (Ellis)

dub-a-dub. rowdydow, rumpus, scuffle, fight.

dub up. pay up.

dubbin' and **plashin'.** see **hedge.**

duds. clothes. 2 rags.

dugs. teats.

dumb-well. a cess-pool. 2 a well dug down to the chalk.

dummel, dummy. dull-witted, silent. 2 dull-edged (of a tool).

dumpish. low-spirited.

dumps. moods, sulks: 'None o' yer dumps 'ere, child.' 2 depression: 'Take no notice of 'er dumps.'

dumpy. stumpy, short and fat. 2 witless.

dunderin'. clumsy, blundering.

dunderpate, dunder-'eaded. a stupid fellow.

dung'll, dun-gel (hard g)**, dung'll-ole.** manure-heap.

dunnekin. privy; outside toilet.

dunnies. coltsfoot leaves, dried to make tobacco.

dure. to endure.

durin'. lasting: 'A good durin' bit o' stuff as'll sarve 'e a life-time.'

dust. a small quantity. **not-so-dusty,** in fair condition: ''ow did yer 'taters turn out?' 'Not ser dusty a'ter all.'

dyke. ditch: 'February fill dyke.' (Old saying.) 2 the bank of a ditch.

E

e. I (short i) often spelt e: ''e be pleased to see ye, that 'e be.' 2 he. 3 ye.

earnt, arnt. earned.

easy-as-pie. easily done.

eat. to taste: 'The pork eats sweet an' frim.'

edderin', eddowin'. heathering, in layering a hedge, the process of securing the upright stakes by twisting in and out willow, briar or ash-shoots. See **hedge.**

'edge-pooper. hedge sparrow. See also **sparrer.**

ef. if.

effs, ewts. efts, newts: dry-effs, lizards, wet-effs, newts.

eft-crop. after or tail crop. See also **a'termath.**

egal. equal.

egg on. to incite.

either, neither. pronounced with long e: 'Thou art lew (luke-warm), nether cold, nether hot.' (Wycliffe, *New Testament*)

eke, eche. to use sparingly.

elber-room. space: 'My soul hath elbow room.' (Shakespeare, *King John*)

eller, ellern. elder tree.

ellum. elm: 'We use' ter make farm-rowlers (rollers) out o' ellum stubs.'

elve, ulve. the handle of a pick axe, etc.

'em. originally hem, them, used by Chaucer and Wycliffe: 'And he axed hem (asked them) ... and he said to hem, whom scien (say) ye that I am?' (Wycliffe's Bible, 1382)

empt. to empty.

en. him: 'Gi' 'en a shoove oop.'

end, eend. the end of a road or track, often found in place names: Dane End, Falconer's End, etc.

endship. a remote dwelling or cluster of dwellings at the end of a way of lower status than a hamlet: 'An inn, inship or endship, homeliest of words, fraught with the significant and tender meaning underlying home.' (A. Jackson)

engine. (pronounced injin), an appliance: 'A certain engine called a net, to kill or destroy game.' 'An engine called a snare.' (Herts Sessions Rolls, 1811)

eno', enow. enough. See also **anough**.

enormious. enormous.

er. before: 'Er it were day.' (Chaucer)

errywig. earwig, see also **arwig**.

etch. stubble.

etch-crop. alternative crop where a previous one has failed.

ever, iver a one, also **arra.** every one, some, any, any at all.

every each or **etch.** each one: 'And everich of us take his aventure.' (Chaucer, *Knight's Tale*) 2 every other one.

everlastin'. constantly: 'Fer ever-lastin' naggin' an 'ocksin' a'ter me.'

eye. to look at: 'The way the bobby eyed 'im med 'im turn 'ot an' cold.' 2 see **island**.

faber. a worker in hard metals.

fa-er. fear. 2 mistake: 'Make no fa-er, ef I says I'll do ut, I'll do ut.'

fag, also **bag.** to cut corn, etc. **baggin' in the haulm,** cutting the high stubble.

fag end. remnant.

faggin' or **baggin' hook.** implement heavier than a sickle, used to cut corn close to the ground.

faggit-bandin'. lovers' manner of walking with their arms round one another's waists.

faggitin' hook. a chopping bill used by woodmen when making up faggots.

faggits. faggots of wood. 2 mischievous children: 'A pa'cel o'yoong faggits, that's what ye are.' 3 ill-behaved untidy old women. 4 a Hertfordshire dish, resembling rissole or sausage.

fain. glad: 'A po'r man be fain o' little.' (Old saying)

faint. a smell, unpleasant, sickly.

fair. gentle. 2 just. 3 fine.

fair, fairish. moderately well: 'I be on'y (only) fairish.' 2 fair-haired:

> 'Fair and foolish, little and loud,
> Long and lazy, black and proud,
> Fat and merry, lean and sad,
> Pale and pettish, red and bad.' (Old rhyme)

fair to middling. answer to a query about one's health; OK.

fall. autumn.

falling ground. slope of a hill: 'Don't niver trot a 'oss on fallin' ground.' (Hertfordshire saying)

fambly. family.

famishin'. very hungry.

fancy. reason or lack of reason: 'I can't tell 'e the fancy o't.'

fannons. short linen sleeves worn by butchers.

fantigue. state of excitement, fuss.

fard'n. farthing.

fare. to go on, to feel: ''ow ev ye bin farin' sin I seed yer last?' 'I aint fared noothin' extry. I aint no great matters these days.'

farnicatin'. smooth-tongued, deceitful, fawning.

fash. to afflict, offend.

fashious. tiresome.

fast. deep, sound: 'Moe like 'issen, 'e sims, an' 'evin a good fast sleep.'

fast by. close to, near.

faather, fayther. father. Faa'er an' mo'er, father and mother (West Herts).

favour. to resemble in appearance.

fear-nothing. a leather jacket, daddy-longlegs.

feart, feared, a-feared. afraid.

Febery, Febewary. February.

feesh. fish (N.E. Herts only).

fein. (pronounced fain), bracken.

feinin'. to cut bracken: 'Le's goo a-feinin'.'

feld, fild, also **mead.** field (N.E. Herts).

fell, fall. to cut down a tree. 2 the skin of an animal.

'fend. to give offence: 'I'll 'ev it out w'th 'em, 'fend or no 'fend.'

fer. for; **fer ter,** to: ''e es gorn fer ter 'list fer a so'dier.' See **for.**

fer, ferder. far, farther.

fer. for fear of: 'I dassent goo be the medder fer the bullocks.'

fer all. notwithstanding.

fer everlastin'. all the time.

fer why. for what reason: 'I'll tell 'e fer whoy ...'

ferritin', ferretin'. prying: 'Ther ye goo agin! Al'us (always) a-ferritin' in other folks' business.'

ferruckin'. fidgetting, scratching: 'Ther's that dog a-ferruckin' on the door again.'

fetch. to give, fetch.

fet, fotch. fetched: 'I fotch 'im a stinger' (I hit him hard).

fettle, feckle. in a good heart (of land).

feu. a small quantity: '''er sint me a feu broth ... a feu porridge.'

few, a goodish few. a considerable number.

fiddle. twiddle.

fi-er. fire:

> 'Jeremiah, blow the fi-er,
> Puff, puff, puff,
> Send the flames a little 'igher,
> Send the cinders out o'the winders,
> Puff, puff puff.' (Old rhyme)

fierce. lively, vigorous: 'A fine strong baby and fierce as a maggit.'

fift. fifth.

figurin'. to do sums. **figure up** or **out,** to consider and come to a conclusion: 'I've bin figurin' on't up, an' I reckon I'll ev nowt t' do w'th it.'

find. to supply.

findy. plentiful:

> 'A cold May and a windy
> Makes a full barn and a findy.' (Old saying)

fine rain. gentle rain.

fit. feet. 2 fought. 3 adapted, ready.

Men of Chorleywood who had enlisted for the army in 1914: ''e es gorn fer ter 'list fer a so'dier.'

fitch. vetch: 'The fitches are beaten out with a staff.' (*Old Testament*)

fitful. uncertain: 'A fitful marnin', proper Aperl weather.'

flack. to comb. 2 to beat with a flail. **flackin',** quick, sharp movements.

flail, frail. flails were made with an ash-pole and a swingel (soft g) or threshel of crab-apple wood or ash, hinged with a leather thong. See **thrail**.

fleet. shallow. To plough fleet, to make a shallow furrow. 2 to skim the cream from milk. 3 skim milk.

flints. hard stones which in parts of Hertfordshire cover the surface of the soil on chalky land: 'Ef ye rake off they flints, ye'll niver git another crap (crop); the land 'ould be ruinated! Ther's m'ister (moisture) under 'em. What's mo', ther's a seed o'fi-er in ivry one on'em t' kip the ground waarm.' (Chauncy believed that this seed of fire accounted for the fertility of flint-covered land.)

flummox. to bewilder.

flummoxed. flustered.

folk. singular and plural, of recent years, and incorrectly, folks.

foller. follow. 2 fallow ground.

foot of the hill. the bottom.

footling. horse's hoof-print. 2 small-minded.

for. a superfluous preposition used as a prefix to verbs: 'He come fer t' break th' bad news.' 'What went ye out for to see?' (*New Testament*)

for'ard, fur'ard. forward. **for'ard** and **latter'd,** early and late.

forestall. to cut (and steal) corn before it is quite ripe: 'Forestalling the wheat with intent to sell.' (Herts Sessions Rolls)

for'oss, for'us. trace-horse or leader in a team (see horse). **for'ost,** foremost.

forsook. forsaken.

fother. fodder.

fo-ur, fower. four: 'A cottage must have fower acres of land laid unto it.' (Statute of Elizabeth: Herts Sessions Rolls, 1670)

fox. to pretend, deceive.

frail. a rush basket.

frazzle. harassed: 'worn to a frazzle'.

free. friendly.

fresh. newly.

fright. any object intended to alarm: 'The children lay a fright in my bed t' gi' me a start.'

frim. strong, luxuriant. 2 succulent: 'Sweet an' frim th' pork ate, too.'

frith, thrift. a coppice or large wood.

frith-fright. thin and scrubby timber.

fritten. to frighten. **frit,** frightened.

fro', frum. from.

frock. dress. See also **smock.** The word frock was always used for dress.

froo. fro: 'to an' froo fro' marn ter night.'

fror, frorn. frozen.

frousty. stale smelling; musty.

furiner. anyone from outside Hertfordshire, particularly from the 'Sheres'. **gooin' furin,** to go into the shires.

furrage. rummage around.

fust. first. **fust on,** at first.

fut. foot.

fuzz, fuzzen, also **fein.** furze.

fuzzenin'. cutting furze: 'Us be gooin' a-fuzzenin', wull 'e coom along-a we?'

G

gaam, graum, gaum. grime. 2 to smear.

gab. to chatter, talk idly: 'I n'arn not leste to gabbe' (I take no pleasure in talking idly: Chaucer).

gad. to go from place to place as opposed to biding at home: 'A lazy 'uzzy! 'er thinks o' nothin' o'ny ter goo gaddin' about.'

gaffer. an old man. 2 an overseer or foreman: ''owsom'-ever, we mun bide by it till sech time as we can ax yer gaffer what it be' (overheard at Watford, 1942). The speaker, an old husbandman, meant: 'We can't do anything about it until we ask the foreman.' 3 grandfather.

gain. stingy, acquisitive. 2 straight, direct: 'the gainest way.'

gainly. dexterous, handy.

gal. girl.

gallas. gamekeeper's trophy tree (gallows) for vermin.

gallus. very, exceedingly. 2 mischievous, rascally, wicked.

games. besides the games which children play everywhere, were Bandy, Bull in the ring, Here goes a shot, Chickens hot – boil the pot, Dabbers or dabstones, Hoopers hide, Fool fool come to school, Here come three dukes a-riding, Pitchers, Cat and kitten, Mivvies or Murries (marbles), Peg-top, Molly Peg, Nagtail, P.P. and the round O., Shinny, Jolly Miller, Warnings.

gamesome. playful.

gammer. used for grandmother and godmother.

gammy. lame. (Welsh *cam*, crooked, hence a game leg.)

gap. a break or opening. 2 a pass between hills.

gape, garp. to stare with open mouth.

gardin, also **archard.** garden.

garland. a wreath of flowers made of wood, wax, silk, feathers, etc., carried by young girls at funerals and subsequently hung in the church. A garland preserved in the Watch Loft, St. Albans Abbey, was said to have been carried at the funeral of Sir Ralph de Rayne, who was murdered when on the way to his wedding in the Abbey. His bride was Lilian Grey, a ward of Sopwell Nunnery.

garm, grarm. messy: 'all garmed up'.

garner, grinery. granary: 'He will pourge his floore and gadre the wheet into his garner.' (Tyndale's *New Testament*, 1526)

garnish-money. demand of 4s 6d to buy beer, made by prisoners in gaol of newly-committed offenders. (Herts Sessions Rolls)

gen'ly. generally, **mos' gen'ly al'ays:** 'Do you always come home sober, George?' 'Mos' gen'ly al'ays I doos, sir.'

gether, gadder. to gather.

ghoost, ghoostes, ghoosteses. ghost, ghosts.

girn. to snarl like a dog, grin.

gittin' on (of time): 'It's gittin' on: I mun be gooin'.'

give, gi'. give. **gi'me, gi'it me, gi't'ere,** give it to me, but when some article is specified, give *us* is used: 'Give us th' 'ammer.' 'Gi'us a 'and w'th th' ladder.'

give, guv, gin, gon. gave: 'Squire gon me a 'arf a crownd.' 2 to thaw: 'Th' frost wunt 'old: it's on the give: it ull give be marnin'.'

give o-er. stop, leave off.

glare. to stare: 'Swiche (such) glaring eyen (eyes) hadde he as an hare.' (Chaucer, *Prologue*)

glib, glip. bright, shiny.

glint. glimpse.

go. to walk as opposed to ride on horseback: 'So mote (might) I ride or go.' (Chaucer)

gobbet. piece, fragment, mouthful.

God's peace. tranquillity: 'Coming in God's peace from St. Andrews.' (Hine, *Hitchin Worthies*)

god-stones. small pebbles, transparent or opaque, carried in the pocket for luck.

going. walking: 'He fell from running to going, and from going to clambering upon his hands and knees.' (*Pilgrim's Progress*)

go'lin. gosling.

gollop. a gulp: 'Take a gollop o'waater an' the pill ull goo down.' 2 to swallow without masticating.

goo. to go: "ullo, Tom, wheer be ye gooin'?' 'I aint a-gooin' nowheers.' 'That ye be.' 'I be not. I're a coomin' back.' 2 a surprising situation: "ere's a rum goo.'

goo aan 'oome. go on home.

goo at. to set about, to work at: 'What be I ter goo at t'morrer?' 'Ye kin ev a goo at the 'taters.' 'Right ye are an' goo'noight ter ye.'

goo-gatus. go to get us: 'The boys be bramble-berryin', (picking blackberries), the gals be gone a-nuttin', you an' me ull goo-gatus some birdseed (plaintain) fer po'r old canaary bird.'

goo on at. to scold, nag.

goo on the parish. to receive parish relief.

good an' all. for ever.

gooin' on. nearly, almost: "e's gooin' on eighty.'

goodman, goodwife, goody. titles of husbandmen and their wives.

good'un. an improbable statement: 'that's a good 'un.'

goold. gold: 'For all the goold in the Spanish mines I wunt do it. (Old saying.)

goosegobs. gooseberries.

goot. goat: 'A voyse (voice) he hadde as small as hath a goot.' (Chaucer, *Prologue*)

gorkin' (?galkin'). walking unwillingly: 'They're took an' ploughed up the nigh cut (short cut), ser now we 'ev ter goo gorkin' round be the road.'

gorn. gone. **gorn dead,** dead: 'Ye dun't keer noothin' fer thim as is gorn dead, an' wery little fer thim as is alive.'

gorn on. become of: 'What's gorn on ol' Nobby?' "e's dead.'

gound. gown.

grin, grind. to show, grind or gnash the teeth: 'Aye, ye med grin! I'll make 'e grin a t'other side o' yer mouth when I gets a 'olt on yer.'

grint. past participle of **grin** and **grind**.

grin'-stun. grindstone.

grizel. a white-haired old person.

grizzle. to fret, grumble, whine: 'What's oop? What be grizzlin' fer now? Ye've bin on the grizzle all day.'

groche, grouch. to complain, murmur.

ground. an enclosed field, land going with a farm.

grouns'l. groundsill; threshold.

grub. food: 'I ne'r seed nob'dy gollop ther grub down like 'im.' 2 a dirty child: 'Come 'ere, ye liddle grub! What 'ev ye bin about?'

grufty. dirty, unwashed, particularly neck and face.

'guisers. (from disguise), mummers.

gumption. resourcefulness, shrewdness.

gunpowlder. gunpowder. Gunpowder mixed with lard was the common Hertfordshire remedy for broken knees in a horse.

gyppo. gypsy: 'T'other day, as I was gooin' to markit w'th maaster in 'is gig, we seed a yong gyppo a-carryin' a dead duck. "Will 'e buy me duck sir," says 'e, "me fine fat duck?" "Gi' 't 'ere," says maaster, an' takin' it in 'is 'and, 'e axed the gyppo 'ow 'e come by't. "I come by't honest, sir, I brung it up from the egg, so I did." "Coom 'ere," maaster says, "look a 'ere," an' 'e showed 'im a bit o' string cut off at the duck's bill, an' th' t'other end leading down its throat. "Ye don't want to tell me," says maaster, "don't I know yer tricks an' 'ow ye fish fer ducks w'th a lump o' bait on yer line? Nip up be'ind," says maaster, "an' I'll drive 'e t' th' p'leece-station," but be that toime, the yong gyppo'd took to 'is 'eels an 'was 'arf-way to Bedf'dsheer. An' the bobbies 'ad the duck ... come to that I could a done w'th it meself, howsiver.'

H

The 'H' was generally silent in speech.

haberdasher. originally in Herts a seller of hats.

habitation. a habitable place. 2 children's 'pretend' homes out of doors.

hackle. outer skin: 'The slug slips his outer skin: what we call his hackle in Hertfordshire.' (Ellis)

hackney. an ambling horse or pad.

had or **ed do.** should do, should have done: 'I aint watered th' 'oss: did I ough'ter ev?' 'Ye 'ed do, an' ye know wery well ye did ough'ter ev.'

haggle-cart. cart (and horse) hired for odd jobs.

haggler. see **higgler.**

half, better be'alf. much better.

hammer on't. the conclusion of a matter, correct solution.

handy-dandy. a covert bribe.

hang. meaning, knack.

hanger. a wood on a slope; originally a slope, wooded or not.

hankicher, onkicher. handkerchief.

hant, aint. have or had not.

hap'orth. halfpenny-worth: 'A pen'orth 'ere an' a 'a'porth there.'

happ'n. perhaps, supposing: ''appen you know better'n yer elders?' 'Maps (perhaps) I do.'

happ'n on. to meet by chance: 'ef I appens on 'im ... ef I appen t' light on 'im, 'e'd bes' look out.'

happen-lucky. to be lucky.

hard. heard.

hardly, don't 'ardly. scarcely: 'I don't 'ardly know.'

Harfordsheer. Hertfordshire.

harrer. harrow: 'When a chap's down, dun't drar the 'arrer o-er 'im.'

harrup. to scratch, dig.

harvest. The harvest-horn was blown at 4.30 a.m. by the farmer; at 5 the men assembled. From dawn to dusk men and women worked together in the harvest fields. 'When the reaping of the last cornfield was all but finished, a small patch of grain was left standing, which was tied or plaited together to form a sheaf, at which the reapers threw their sickles, competing for the honour of the last cut. In some places this ceremony, accompanied by shouting, was called Crying the Neck (Scandinavian *nek*, a sheaf). Crying the Mare was a noisy song of triumph over farmers who were late in getting in the harvest.'

Crying the Mare (each line is repeated 3 times):
'I have her.'
'What have ye?'
'A Mare.'
'Who's be she?'
'Farmer ...... ' (the master's name).
'Where'll us send her?'
'To Farmer ...... ' (naming the dilatory neighbour).

The last sheaf, often called the Corn Baby, trimmed with flowers, was lifted to the last load; the wagon and the horses were decorated, the horsekeeper had the honour of driving,

Little Hadham church, seen across a field where the corn stands in shocks after the harvest. (Mrs Amy Coburn)

men and boys ran alongside, carrying boughs of ash and singing:

> Master he's got in his corn,
> Well mawn (mown), well shorn,
> Ne'er heeled over, ne'er stuck fast,
> The harvest has come home at last.

About Hinxworth they sang as the last load reached the farm:

> Hip hip hurrah, harvest home,
> Three plum-puddings are better than none,
> So hip hip hurrah, harvest home.

Here the farm wenches would run out and pour water over the men amid shouts and merriment. This ceremony was supposed to ensure a good crop for the following year. After that beer and bread and cheese were provided for all.

The harvest-home supper, called in Hertfordshire the Hockey, was the great event of the year, when 'the master and the missus', the men with their wives and children feasted and drank together, sang harvest songs and later, when the tables were cleared away, danced the old country dances in the decorated barn.

haulms, hums. stalks of potatoes, beans, etc.

haulmin'. to clear high stubble with a sickle.

haunt. abode.

hay-abouts. raw recruits of the Herts militia who wore a hayband on the right and a straw band on the left leg, as they could not tell right from left. The sergeant ordered: Hay-about, straw-about, instead of right, left.

hay-cutter. a man who went from farm to farm to cut and bind trusses from the rick. He carried a scimitar-shaped knife. Also called **hay-binder**.

haymaking. In old days and given good weather, the grass was cut towards the end of June and carried on the fourth day. The four day routine produced the super-excellent hay which, according to Lamb, scented the London streets, borne on the wind from Hertfordshire fields.

HAYING IN EAST HERTS: The old and very particular way of haymaking before the age of machinery, and subject to ideal June weather, contributed by the late Archibald Jackson.

'You aks (ask) me to tell ye 'ow we went a-'ayin' in our parts in them o'd days wi' the scythe an' the rake, wi' th' 'osses pullin' th' mower an' th' tedder. Well, thisyer [this is a pure old-Saxon single word, *theser*(a), which is wrongly written today as if it were this-here] wus the proper way on 't. You must onder-stand we wus up a troifle for'arder than ord'ny toimes, so as we c'd git a bite o' summut afore startin' from 'oome, an' p'raps a drop o' small beer wi' 't, an' so's we wus in the field be six o'clock sharp, ready t' start mowin'. The leadin' mower – we called 'im the lord [in the middle ages the leader or lord was called by the Latin word, *messor*, reaper] – was moostly the hade (head) 'osskeeper an' ploughman, an' when we'd all sharped our scythes wi' th' rubstone as we cyarried (carried) on our rizers [a leathern holder 'stringed over the lumber'] an' set the bales [withs (withies) bent in a semi-circle at the head of the scythe and fastened to the handle, helping to carry a heavy swathe of grass and preventing it from falling off as the mower swung his scythe, until the windrow was reached] roight, pertickler if t'wus a full crop.

Out steps th' lord t' cut th' first few swarthes, an' sets the swing on the strooak (stroke) fer th' tothers t' foller 'im, oone a'ter th' tother an' as cloose (close) be'ind as is saafe. Come eight o'clock we cried off an sot down to brekfus, wi' moost loike a bottle o' beer atween us. A'ter that, the same mornin' moind ye as the graass as bin cut, in come t' th' fild th' rest o' th' men an' th' women-folk as well, t' ted the graass, be which I mean liftin' of it up wi' th' fork an' shakin' it so as it falls off the tines an' lays quite foine on th' ground round ye, to start it dryin', an' th' saame day they'll tu'n (turn) it oonce or twoice again.

O' coorse this 'aymakin' 'ud ha'e t' be about th' middle o'Jewne (June) an' th' weather just roight fer th' job, fine an' warmish an' all th' better of a little breeze.

The mowers wus quoite ready fer bever at 'leven, brade (bread) an' cheese an' a good swig o'beer apiece out o' th' bottle th' maaster 'ad sent the boy across wi', as wus t' o'd-fashioned waay. Bless me, you could sweat a pint out o' ye ev'ry hour, leastways ev'ry etch (alternate) hour, a mowin' o' graas in 'ay-toime, an' barley in 'arvest.

A'ter bever on they goo while (until) dinner at oone o'clock an' waren't ev'ry body ready fo' 't? Then they staart agin an' goo on come (until) fooer, when 't wur toime fer a few minutes rest an' fooerses t' squench ther thirst agin wi' a drop o'beer. Be that toime, if th' weather'd hilt (held), sawm on 'em'd be raakin' th' grass inter win'rows while sixes comes round, an' th' women-folk then maakes tracks fer 'oom t' git supper ready, an' th' 'aymakers as are left, moostly keep on a bit longer a-raakin' th' grass inter little cocks.

The secon' day th' cocks wus tu'ned (turned) over agin th' wind an' shook out an' built inter baastard cocks as big agin, an' so left fer that noight. The nextest day, the fild was gorn roight through, an' th' 'ay cocked ready fer cyartin'. The foourth day, when t'wus loaded, an' cyarted t' th' stack ur (or) put in th' baarn if ther waan't no fear on't 'eatin. Sweet an' dry an' green as 't should be, an' full o'seed an' Jeune flowers.'

hazel. top soil seen dried and friable (workable).

he, 'im, 'isself, issen. he himself.

head. spring, source. **head of the way,** beginning.

headland, also **hedge-green.** margin of grass next the hedge at the top and bottom of plough-land, on which the ploughman turns his horses. Farm carts also follow the headlands in going from field to field. Possibly these were the old common ways bordering the common land. In North-East Herts the headland, after serving for turning the horses, was ploughed lengthways when the rest of the field was finished.

head-'uns. government officials.

heap. a large quantity: 'The wisdom of an heep of lerned men.' (Chaucer, *Prologue*.)

he-ard. heard.

hear tell on. to hear: 'I've 'e-ard tell on't.'

heart. condition of land: 'In good 'eart.'

hedge, hadge. 'We be main proud o' wer (our) 'edges in 'arfedshere: well set an' well laid (layered) they be: blackthorn an' whitethorn, dogwood an' sloe, 'azel an' crab-stock, 'edge-row trees an' 'edge'ogs ...'

To stag a hedge or to 'bucket of it off,' was to cut it to 3 or 4 ft., or lower, leaving strong stems with a bunch of stubs atop, in fancied resemblance to a buck's or stag's head. A hedge is also 'thetched' or 'edderd' (heathered). This was the binding of the top of the hedge with hazel or bramble. Dubbin' and plashin', to make a smooth surface or to reduce a hedge by striking with an adze; to bend or cut half-through a bough (dubbin') and then weave it among the upright stems (plashin').

hedge'og hedge'oag, hadge'og (N.E. Herts), also called **urchin.** hedgehog. **Hertfordshire hedgehogs,** stunted trees suitable for clubs.

heighths. high ground, hill-tops.

her. she.

hern. (her one) hers. 2 heron: 'Jack-'erns an' Moll-'erns, a-buildin' ther nestes in the 'igh tree-tops.'

het, also **tarre.** to urge, encourage.

hev, hevin, hed. have, having, had: 'I 'ev 'ed.' 2 to get the better of someone.

hider. hither: 'Come hider love to me.' (Chaucer, *Prologue*)

hidin'. beating.

hie. to hasten.

higgler, haggler, heggler, also **badger, kidder, carrier, loader.** a pedlar of eggs, etc.: 'License for John Babb of Hertford to be a common higler, buyer and seller of henns, chickens, capons, eggs, butter, cheese, fish and other dead victuals except pheasants, hares and partridges.' (Herts Sessions Rolls, 1684)

him, her, they. that he, she, they should: 'I'd rather him come alone.'

hinder, hindest. behind, last.

hinder part afore. back to front.

hippin-stones. stepping-stones.

hiptypips an' haaves. hips and haws.

hish. to make a sound to encourage a dog: 'Ther goos a rabbit! 'ish yer dog a'ter 'im.' See **het.**

hit. to strike. 2 to meet with. See **strike.**

hit it. to guess aright.

hit off. to agree. 2 to meet opportunely.

hitch, hatch. link (of a chain). 2 a slight move: ''itch up a bit so's I c'n set aside o' yer.'

ho, whoa. stop.

hoary. frosty.

hob-a-nob. talk with, consort with.

hobblinfut. the cobbling last to be found in every cottage, where the father mended and clumped his family's shoes.

hobbydi'oy. hobbledihoy, between boy and man.

hocktide. Easter Monday and Tuesday.

hocksin', also **tanketin'.** following anyone about: 'I wunt be 'ocksed fro' maarnin' ter night ... tanketin' a'ter me all the while.' 2 to look for: 'Them boys be 'ocksin' birds nestes.' 3 **hocksed,** at a loss, perplexed.

hodod. apple dumpling.

hoddod, hoddydod, hodmandod, hod-me-dod, oddydod, odden-dod, oddy-snail. snail. 2 the empty coloured snailshells found in chalky places. Also **dodman.**

hodmidod. scarecrow, usually one carrying a 'gun.' See **scarecrow.**

hogo. (?haut gout), a strong smell.

ho'd. hold. **holt, hoult, hilt,** held: 'Catch a' 'olt o' the reins.'

holler. hollow, a small wooded ravine. 2 to shout, cry: 'I'll giv' e summut t' 'oller about.'

holp, halp, holpen. helped.

holt. a grove.

hommock. to walk with a clumsy gait.

honest, to do honest. to treat fairly: 'Me brother aint done honest be me.'

honey. a term of affection (young child). 2 a clumsy awkward person.

hong. hung.

hoof. to measure a piece of ground: 'I've put me 'oof o-er it' (I have stepped it out).

hook. an implement. Baggin' or faggin' 'ook, bill'ook, rippin'-(reaping)'ook.

hope. to expect.

horns. the Ceremony of the Horns, supposed to have been a druidical rite, was observed at Hitchin until about 1750.

horrocks. see **shack.**

horse. singular and plural: 'The Horse have stood to helth.' 'The great mortality of our Horse.' (Herts Sessions Rolls)

horse-cries. carter's cries: 'Gee up', 'Jup', come up; ''Old up', 'Wo', 'Wo-back', 'Hait', 'Het', halt.
Ploughboy's cries: 'O-O-Oh-along', come along; 'Gee-up', go quicker; 'Wo', 'Wo-gee', stop; 'Gee-ower', 'Gee-ho', turn

right; 'Come'e wo', 'Come 'ether', turn left. 'Oot back', 'Gee off', 'Gee wut off', warning cry when horses are too much on the near side, the ploughboy, walking to face the team and pointing with his whip to off or near, cried 'Aw'. In later days when the boy walked alongside the thiller, he touched the for'ost (leader) with his whip and cried, 'Come 'ether', turn left, or 'Gee ower', turn right.

Harvest and hay carrying cries: 'Gee up', 'Wo along', go on, cried by the cock-boy; 'Wo-gee', stop, cried by the pitcher; 'Wo Grizel', 'Wo Punch', stop, cried by the cock-boy; 'Come 'ether', turn left; 'Come o-er', 'Gee ower', turn right.

Stableman's cry when calling horses in from the field: 'Ca-ahm along, Ca-ahm along, K'p, K'p, K'p'.

Farm horses' names: Boxer, Captain, Dapper, Di'mond, Duke, Grizel, Jolly, Prince, Punch, Scott: (obsolete) Gegutter, Parrat, Pepper, Salt.

hoss. horse.

hoss-keeper. the man in charge of farm-horses.

hoss-stinger. dragonfly (not horsefly).

hot, hotten. to heat. **hotted,** heated: 'I 'otted 'im some be-er, 'e wer' that co'd.'

hot-ache. the tingling sensation of the fingers after getting very cold.

hotchel. to hurry.

hoult, ho'd. hold.

house, housen (plural). cow-'us, 'en-'us, great-'us, po'r-'us, etc.: 'Housen be better than land tonight.' An old saying on a stormy night.

howlet. see **spence**.

howiver, hawever. a common and irrelevant ejaculation at the end of a sentence.

howsiver, howsomever, howsomdiver. however.

huck-me-buck, hucker-me-buck, hugger-me-buff. the late crop of hay from fields grazed by cattle.

huddles. hurdles.

hue and cry. the pursuit of an offender by the constable and anyone he might call to help him: 'John Waters of Barkhamsted St. Peters ... for refusing to carry a hue and cry in the night when desired by the constable.' (Herts Sessions Rolls, 1686)

huggermugger. to conceal, concealment.

huggle, huckle. to huddle.

hull. to hurl.

hulls. see **ails**.

humble, also **bomble.** bumble-bee.

humblin'. humming, rumbling, growling.

humbuggin. troublesome: 'A proper 'umbuggin job, as the grave-digger said when 'e come down onrespected (unexpectedly) on a skelington.'

hume. hymn or canticle:
> 'King Jarge the second 'ome is come,
> The King 'e 'ev come 'um:
> Together therefore, let us sing
> The hume what's called Te Dum.'
>> By a parish clerk in E. Anglia (borrowed)

hunchin'. shoving: 'The lambs hunchin' and butting.'

hunderd. hundred.

hunk, hunch. a thick slice of bread.

hurlocky. stony chalk: 'a whitish, hurlocky, stony earth.' (Ellis)

husbandman, also **servants in husbandry.** all who work on the land. Chaucer used the word husbandman for the master of the family. In Herts Sessions Rolls, yeoman, farmer and labourer are all husbandmen. They could turn their hand to all kinds of farm-work.
> 'Sometimes I do reap an' sometimes I do mow,
> Sometimes a-hedgin' an' a-ditchin' I do go,
> Ther's nothin comes amiss to me, fro' the harrer
>> (harrow) to the plough,
> An' so I gets me livin', by the swe-at o' me brow.'
>> (Old song)

husbandry. thrift, good management.

hussif. housewife: 2 the needle holdall soldiers were issued with in the First World War.

hussy. a bad woman.

huven. distended (of a sheep).

huver, hover. to ted (shake out) new mown grass.

ifle, isle. to hustle, drive off.

ig'rant. ignorant.

ile, iol. oil.

ill-favoured. evil-looking.

image. resemblance. 2 child. 3 an object, a fright.

imp, impet. a small child.

in. to bring in, to carry: 'In the corn and in the barley.'

in a manner o' speaking. so to say.

in'ards. inside: 'Me innards be all o'a squabble.'

in coorse. of course.

inning the corn. harvest home.

inion. onion.

in years. growing old, approaching a given age: 'The ol' chap's in 'is eighty.' ''Tis a bit ferish on. We're all gittin' on in years.'

I're. (I are), I am: 'I're gooin' t' kill me baconer (pig): I're obleeged t' do ut.'

irksome. wearisome: 'Toime I wus yong ther' waan't no schools: we did wer (our) summin' be a tally an' in wer 'eads. We dint need ter write, we made wer mark an' ol' passon (parson) writ wer names 'long side. New passon's larnin' us t' read, an' proper irksome 'tis. "Jist job along," he says, "an' it'll come suddent-loike!" "T'aint loikely," I says, "not at my toime o' life." I don' 'old wi' sich notions, but 'e's 'igh-church, siminly, an' 'is 'ead's full o' maggits.'

island, also **eye, core.** land partially or entirely surrounded by water.

ivory. ivy.

ivrythink. everything.

jab. thrust.

jabberin men. javelin men who walked beside the judge's carriage as he drove to Hertford Assizes. They wore caped coats over liveries like those worn by the High Sheriff's servants.

jack. any labour-saving contrivance. 2 a candlestick. 3 a revolving clockwork appliance used for roasting meat before a fire.

jack up. to throw up, to leave off.

jack-in-the-green. a man, usually a sweep, hidden in a flower-trimmed wire or withy bell-shaped frame, who danced in May Day games.

jackdaa. jackdaw:

> Says the oul' jackdaa t' the yoong jackdaa,
> As they sot on the fence t' gither,
> Says the oul' jackdaa t' th' yoong jackdaa,
> We be 'evin' raa (raw) fraasty weather.
> Says the yoong jackdaa t' the oul' jackdaa,
> As they sot on the fence t'gether,
> Says the yoong jackdaa t' th' oul' jackdaa,
> We be 'evin' ra-er (rare) tachy weather.
>
> (Old Herts rhyme)

jacketin'. a beating.

jag. a small load or drag of hay. 2 to carry hay, etc.

jallus. to suspect.

j'alous. jealous: 'The man's as j'alous as ol' 'arry.'

jannock. see **jonnock**.

jaw. to talk too much: ''e's all jaw, loike a ship's (sheep's) 'ead.'

jest, jist, jeest. just: 'Do 'ev jist a bit more pudd'n.' 'Well, on'y jeest a tiddy bit.'

jiffle. to be restless.

jiffy. a moment.

jiggle, joggle. to shake.

jiggumbob. gimcrack.

jine. join.

jink. a small waterworn pebble. 2 to chink.

j'ist. joist.

job along. to proceed steadily, to contrive somehow.

jogger. one who plods heavily onward: 'Fellow joggers of the plough.' (Dryden)

jonnock, jannock. fair, honest: 'T'aint jonnock!' It is not fair.

joskins. Hertfordshire bumpkins.

jot. the least bit: 'I dunt keer (care) a jot.'

joult-skull, also **shaven-pate.** a stupid person, originally a bald head.

juniper lecture. see **naggin'**.

jussocks. tufts of grass overlooked in a hayfield: 'They jussocks warn't (were not) tedded (tossed) proper. Give 'em a shake o-er.'

j'y. joy: 'J'y goo w'th 'e.' An ironical farewell.

K

kattern. see **cattern**.

kecks. cow parsley.

keech. to dip for water.

keeper. engagement ring.

kerf. the groove made by a saw: 'In fallin' a tree keep the kerf nigh the ground.'

keroons. cherries, see **croons**.

kibble. of a lame horse, to limp.

kid. to take in. 2 a bundle of six score small faggots. 3 to form pods (peas and beans).

kidder. see **higgler**.

kindly. according to kind. 2 to have a liking.

kin'dom. kingdom. (Kindom, from *cyne*, royal, is the early form of the word.)

kin'red. kindred.

kissing-gate, clap-gate. a small gate hung in a narrow enclosure, through which only one person can pass at a time.

kiver. an oval oaken tub or trough, bound with ashen hoops, used in butter-making.

knocknobbler. see **nobbling stick**.

knoot. knew nought.

knowed, knoo. knew.

L

laastic-sides. boots with elastic at the side: 'I mun buy me a noo pair o' laastic-sides fer Sundays.'

ladder. fore and back extensions of a farm-cart or wagon. See **copses.**

land. the unploughed portion of a field. 2 one ridge and one furrow: 'What cleans the land like a good plough-share and a good man behind the plough?' (Old saying)

lanky. overgrown:

> 'A lanky man is lazy
> He has a stone heart.'
>
> (Old song)

lanthorn. lantern.

lap, hap. to wrap, fold around. **to make a lap,** to turn up skirt or apron for carrying wood, flowers, etc.

larges. (pronounced larjiz), an informal meal of bread and cheese and beer, taken at the end of harvest and bought with money made by the sale of rabbits bolted from the corn. 2 originally a gift of money demanded by the reapers; on receiving it they cried three times, 'Halloo, larges.'

larn. to learn. 2 to teach: 'Learn me true understanding' (Psalm CXIX). 'Schoolmissus larnt me to tell me letters.' 'I'll larn yer,' a common threat. To larn how many beans make five, to learn by bitter experience.

larnin'. education.

larrup. to flog, beat. **larrupin',** a beating.

lat. to let, let.

lattermath. second crop, see also **a'termath.**

lawyers. strong wooden props used to hold up a rick.

lay. a song. 2 to lie down: 'The sheaves down-laying on the floor.' 3 to wager, warrant, predict, to badger: 'She lay at me hard to turn aside.' (*Pilgrim's Progress*) 4 to sleep well: 'How did you sleep?' 'Thank 'e, doctor, I lay wery coomf'table.' 5 to lay (layer) a hedge. 6 to lay holt on, to catch hold. 7 to lay into, to beat.

lay of the land. general features. Also used metaphorically.

laylock. lilac, laylock was the correct pronunciation at one time.

lea. meadow.

lead. to carry a load of hay or corn. **lad,** carried. 2 lead off, to find fault.

leadern. leathern.

leaders. muscles.

leaf. leave: 'The yoong chap es gorn off arout (without) leaf, 'corder to what I 'eers.'

leasing. gleaning.

least, least-un. youngest.

leastways. at least.

leave. to give leave. 2 let: 'Leave goo me arm.'

ledge. range: 'The great ledge of Hills [the eastern Chilterns] crossing the County from Barkshire, called by some the Alps of England.' (Chauncy)

leer. to veer: 'He leered away on the other side as one ashamed.' (*Pilgrim's Progress*)

leerin'. sly: 'leerin' as any ol' fox.'

lend. to hand or pass.

le's. let us.

let. to set: 'They was lettin' the postes inter the groun'.' 2 allow to escape: 'My doll letted her sawdust.'

let fly. (originally to let fly an arrow), to scold, rail: 'The missus come in suddent-like an' din't she jest let fly!'

lew, lew-warm. neither hot nor cold.

libberd. leopard: 'We seed the lions an' the libberds at the fa-ir an' we rid on the merry-goo-roun'.'

licker. poser, problem: ''ow much is 8 times 7? Well, if that aint a licker an' no mistake.'

liddle, lettle, lil. little. Lil, Danish *lille*, small, is not a contraction.

lie. see **lay.**

lief, liefer. rather, in preference:
'The Knight had lever (liefer) for to die,
Than breke his trouth.' (Gower)

light. to alight.

light on. to come across.

like. to like: 'Like 'im! I likes 'im 'bout es mooch es th' deevil likes 'oly waater!' 2 to love (the word love is rarely used): 'I like 'e iver ser mooch, me da-er.' 3 to like fairly well: 'I likes Maery's sister but I likes (love) Maery iver so.' 4 to appreciate: 'Ef ye dun't like me work, say so, an' I'll goo soom-wheers else (elsewhere).' 5 a suffix to adjectives and adverbs: 'Th' young gal med be a bit strange-like jist at fust.'

likely. promising: 'Of'entimes them as sims mos' likely be more likelier than them as sims mos' likeliest.' (An obscure Hertfordshire saying.)

liker. more like, more likely.

limb. youngster, young limb, young fidget, imp.

limber. active.

lingerin', also **longful.** wearing, longing for: 'I're lingerin' fer 'e t' come 'ome, me daer.'

lip. impertinence: 'None o' y'r lip, now.'

lissom. graceful.

lither. supple.

live. to compare, compete: 'That 'oss o' yourn can't live wuth master's noo mare.'

loaden. laden: 'The fields loaden with good crops.'

loader. see **higgler**.

lob, tob. to throw a small object a short distance.

lock-up. see **cage**.

lollop. to slouch.

look. to expect.

look-'ere. a usual beginning to a sentence.

look-see. to search: ''ere, boy, look-see ef ye kin find a two-three eggs in th' 'en-'us.'

loomy. of thick tenacious clay (not of loam).

loony. lunatic.

loop. the winding of a river.

loopy. silly, stupid.

loppetin'. shambling along in small forward movements: 'I seed a two-three rabbits loppetin' along.'

lord. the leader of the mowers. See **haymaking**.

lord of the harvest. 'Some stayed, sober working-man who understands all sorts of Harvest-work. If he be of able body, he commonly leads the swarth in reaping and mowing.' Tusser.

lousy. verminous: 'Lousy as a cuckoo.'

love. see **like**.

love-apples. tomatoes.

love-child. more often bastard, an illegitimate child. According to the Herts Sessions Rolls, the mother of a bastard was committed to prison for one year.

lovely, loverly, loovly. lovely, darling.

lovyer. lover: 'A lovyere and a lusty bacheler.' (Chaucer.)

'lowance. allowance, share (see **bever**). 2 to deal out: 'The missus (farmer's wife) 'lowanced out the tea an' sugar.'

lucifers, also **tanstickers.** brimstone matches.

lucky, to happen lucky. to be fortunate.

lug. to pull along.

luggin' birds nestes. to take nests.

lurk, a touch of the lurk. malingering, work-shy.

M

ma', me'. may. **me'be,** may be.

maan't. may not.

maam. (mahm), ma'am.

mag. chatter.

maggits. maggots. 2 absurd ideas.

main. very: 'I be main glad ter 'ear it.'

make bold. to dare: 'I med bould t' goo ter Squi-er isself...'

make like. to seem about to ...: 'That chap's a porcher right 'nough! I see 'im las' night be th' spinney: 'e made like 'e wus 'evin' a Sunday walk, but 'is puggy (ferret) wus workin' the rabbit-bank fer 'im an' 'is tarrier waitin' fer the rabbits t' bolt.'

malling. meowing of a cat.

mammerin', maumerin'. the small noise made by bats.

mammet, mommet, maumet. an image, idol. 2 see **scarecrow**.

manner. sort: 'That chap ben't no manner o' use.' **all manner o' what,** jumble. **in a manner o' speakin',** so to say.

many's the time. often.

marnin'. good morning: 'Fine marning,' 'cold marnin',' etc., the usual Hertfordshire greeting.

marvles. also **mivvies** and **murries,** marbles.

massy. mercy.

master, the master. the head of the house, employer. 2 **mas'r,** usual but not universal title of all married husbandmen, unmarried men of any age being called by their Christian names or nicknames. 3 chief: master-cow, leader of the herd; master-shoot, leading shoot of a tree.

masterful. bossy.

masty, mastiffy-dog. mastiff.

mate. used by a husband to his wife; a pal.

mated. worn out, confused: 'One trooble a'ter anoother till I'm reg'lar mated.'

mathered. bothered.

matters, no great matters. not well in health.

maulkin, maukin, mawks. a girl. 2 a slattern: 'Ye lazy great mauks, you!' 3 a mop. 4 a **scarecrow.** 5 a May-baby (doll).

maumet. an idol.

maw. stomach: 'This boy has been tampering with something that lies in his maw undigested.' (*Pilgrim's Progress*)

mawerkin'. messing.

mawker. oven-mop made of rag.

may. maiden.

may be. is: 'What time may it be?'

Mayers. children who went a-maying on May-day. They carried boughs and flowers and sometimes a May-baby (a doll), going from house to house singing the Mayers' songs.

mazed. bewildered.

mazzards. cherries. See **croons**.

mead. field, see **feld**.

a meal o' wittles. any meal.

meals of husbandmen:

6 a.m.	fust brakfus' or brefus.
8 a.m.	secon' brefus.
10 or 11 a.m.	bever, 20 minutes break for beer or beer 'n bren-chaze. 'lowance, a bever provided by the master.
12 p.m.	dinner, 1 hour's break.
4 p.m.	fourses, originally called bever or cheesin-time.
6 p.m.	sixes, beer.
After work	supper.

meat. food of all kinds: 'God never sends mouths but he sends meat.' (Tusser) **manger meat,** cattle food.

med, moot, mote, mout. might: 'Rat catcher med coom terday er (or) 'e mootn' coom afore termorrer.' 'Ye mote es well a (have) done it fust es laast.'

meller. mellow: 'A meller bit o' bacon.'

member, mimber. to remember.

membrers. men and boys with blackened faces who carried a guy on November 5th:

> 'Please t' rimimber
> The fift' o' Novimber,
> Goonpouldre, tr'a'son an' plot.'

merries. (mérises), sweet black cherries, better known as Hertfordshire blacks. See also **croons**.

mesh. mash.

mess. hot bread and milk.

messin' about. wasting time, doing nothing in particular.

mettle. spirit, anger.

midden, middings. dunghill.

middlin'. medium: 'A middlin' size'. 2 bad: 'A middlin' bit o' work! Coun't ye do better'n that ef ye tried a bit 'arder?' 3 fairly well in health: 'Perty middlin', thenk'ee.' 4 not well: 'er's on'y middlin' terday.'

midsty. the threshing floor or space between two mows in a barn.

miggle. middle.

mighty. very, exceedingly.

mile. singular and plural: 'ow fer? gittin' on fer three mile?'

A few mischievious yoong magpoys on Fore Street, Hertford one morning c.1906; one has been sent to fetch a pail of milk for his mother but is more interested in the photographer.

Miles's boy. a fictitious name for a tale-bearer: 'I wun't 'ear a word agin my maaster, an' I dunt keer (care) 'oo tolt yer, Miles's boy or not.'

mind. intention. 2 to look out. 3 to take care of. 4 to remember: 'Master ev a mind ter let th' yoong bull out ... mind yerself, ye can't troost 'im.' 'Ther's the gal as minds Parson's childern: 'oller ter 'er t' goo back.' 'I mind th' time as bulls olus (always) rin (ran) in th' medder 'long o' th' cows.'

mint. a great deal: 'Th' 'ol' man mun ev a mint o' money put away somewheers.'

mirry, murry, merry. **a mirry day,** pleasant weather.

mischief. harm: 'He threw a chair at me and narrowly escaped doing me a mischief.' (Herts Sessions Rolls) 2 a child or person who plays pranks: 'Was ther iver sich a mischief! Stop yer antics! 'A' done, now, do!'

mischievious. mischievous: 'I'll ev ter tiake me stick to them boys ... mischievious yoong magpoys.'

misery. a miserable object, animal or child.

miss, mess. failure.

the missus. the lady of the house. 2 the farmer's wife. 3 missus, the usual name for a man's wife (also me mate, me boss and me ol' wuman): 'Wer iver ev ye got ter, missis? I're bin 'ollerin' a'ter yer a 'alf 'n 'ower 'n more.'

mister. trade, occupation, craft: 'What mister men?' (men of what occupation: Chaucer).

'In youthe he lerned hadde a good mister,
He was a wel good wrighte, a carpenter.'

(Chaucer, *Prologue*)

misure. measure.

mite. anything very small. 2 no good at all: 'taint a mite o'good.'

mivvies. marbles, see **marvies.**

mizmaze, mizzy-mozzy. confusion.

mizzle. to drizzle. 2 to slink away.

mo, moe, moo, mo-er, 'mer. more: 'And nevere mo he shall his lady see.' (Chaucer, *Knight's Tale*) 'Send out moe horses.' (Shakespeare, *Macbeth*) 'Moo than XIJ legions of Angelles.' (Tyndale's *New Testament*) More and most are often used with comparative and superlative adjectives: 'More sharper than your swords.' (Shakespeare) 'More oftener than not.' 'The most coldest Christmas as iver I remimber.'

mo-arn, moorn. to mourn.

moggy. an oddly dressed woman. 2 a common name for a cat. 3 pet name for any young animal.

moil. to work as a drudge.

m'ist, m'isty. moist, damp:
> 'A misty, m'isty marnin'
> When cloudy was the weather.'

monch. to munch, chew.

mooch, mouch. to loaf, hang about, pry, act in a suspicious way.

moon. 'the moon waxes and wanes; a rising and a shrinking moon.'

moot. may, must, might. 'He moot ben deed' (dead). (Chaucer)

mort. a large number: 'A mort o' folk.'

moournin'. mourning: 'All stinted (ended) is the moorning and the teres.' (Chaucer, *Knight's Tale*)

mortal. exceeding: 'It's a mortal shame!' 'Be n't it mortal strange?' 2 'No mortal use,' not the least use.

mo'sel. morsel, a small quantity or thing: 'The baby's got the 'oopin'-cough, po'r lil mo'sel.'

'most. almost, mostly. **most neen** (most on end), usually, more often than not. **most an end,** a long time: 'I was with him most an end.'

mot, motty. a mark to shoot at.

mote, moit. may, might.

to go motherin'. to visit one's mother, especially on Mothering Sunday (mid-Lent): 'I'm going a-motherin' come Sunday, with a simnel (cake) for a present, same as always. Mother will have made frumenty, and gra'mer will toss a carlin (pancake) and we'll be real happy ...'
> 'I'll to thee a Simnel bring,
> 'Gainst thou go a-mothering,
> So that when she blesses thee,
> Half that blessing thou'lt give me.'
>   (Herrick)

mouldy, mowldy. friable soil, nice to handle.

mound. an artificial hillock.

mount. a mounting or horse-block.

mouse. a term of affection. 2 **meece, meeces,** mice: 'We be pested wuth meece. Th' 'ouse be tainted with meeces.'

> Ash'ell po'r people,
> Sot on the Church steeple,
> A-crackin' o'meece
> With a five-farden beetle.

> (Old rhyme of Ashwell, Herts.)

mow. the place in a barn on either side of the midsty, where the corn or barley is heaped before it is threshed. 2 the heap itself.

much, mucher. of use: 'Thet ol' 'unter'll niver be a mucher fer kerridge work.' **much of a mucher,** a dishonest person. **much of a muchness,** alike.

muck. dung: 'Money is like muck, not good except it be spread.' (Bacon) 2 sweat. **muck out,** to clean: 'See you muck out the steadings, Jarge.' To **come a mucker,** to fall, literally and metaphorically.

mucky. dirty.

muddle (about). to do little work.

mug. face, mouth, grin. 2 fool.

muggin. fat.

muggle. muddle.

muggy, mungy. warm, damp (weather).

mum. silent.

mumblin' an' chunterin'. muttering, going on about something.

mumprin', cock-a-mumprin'. showing off.

mun. must.

mung. to mix.

munt, munno', mount, maant, mus'n'. must not.

murry. merry. **murries,** marbles, see **marvles**.

musheroon. mushroom.

muster (Mr.). So and so, used when speaking to or of squire, parson and steward or bailiff.

mystery. see **mister**.

N

naa'ty. naughty.

nab, nob, nobble. to seize. 2 to acquire dishonestly. 3 to tamper with.

nacherly. naturally.

nag. a saddle horse or any horse other than farm horses.

naggin'. a prolonged carping, also called a **juniper lecture,** juniper wood burning longer than other woods.

nailpaster. (passer), a gimlet.

namo, namore. no more.

nappy. strong.

nary. ne'er a. **narra,** not any, none. **nary woon on 'em,** not one of them.

natur'. nature. **nat'ral,** natural.

natty. neat, spruce. 2 clever.

naun. none or nothing: ''e's naun but a boy: dunt ye be ser 'ard on 'im.'

nauthin', noothin'. nothing.

nay. no, in answer to a direct question.

near. see **nigh,** not far distant in time or place: 'Near on three mile.' 2 miserly, stingy: 'Th' o'd man is that near 'e wunt spend a penny ef a 'alfpenny'll do.'

ne'bour. neighbour.

neckid. naked. **neckid snail,** a slug.

needs-cost. of necessity, at any cost.

ner. nor. 2 near. 3 than: 'God's help is nearer ner the fair even(ing).' (Old saying)

nest, neest. (plural es): 'Ther's a many sart o'neestes: ther's birds' an' wapses' an pissums' (ants) neestes, an' ther was ol' Job, 'im in the Bible, 'e 'ad a neest an' 'e 'oped as 'e'd die in it.'

never a one. none.

next. nearest.

nexun. the size of: ''Twer red an' round an' nexun a apple.'

a nice bit. a considerable time or size.

nicely. pretty well, improving in health.

nicket, nick, snick. a small cut or notch: 'Nigh as a nicket,' also 'nigh as nick it.' 2 to cheat, steal.

niggardy-piggardy. stingy.

niggle. to spend time over trifles. **niggling,** small, mean.

nigh. near. **well nigh,** all but: 'It well nigh bruck 'is heart.'

nigh and nearly. almost: ''Tis nigh and nearly five o'clock.' 2 close.

nigh cut. a short cut.

nim. quiet, careful:
'Me lord rides jim, jim, jim (jingling),
Me lady rides nim, nim, nim (quietly).'

nip in, out, off. to move quickly: 'Nip off out o' 'ere.' 2 a short steep rise in the road or ground. 3 a limited quantity: 'O'd powny gits a nip o' grass gooin' along the lanes.'

nis, nisn. is not: 'I tell 'e ther nisn namoe.'

nit. egg of a parasite: 'Dead as a nit.'

niver. never.

no danger! No fear!

no how, also **no sense.** not in any way: 'I can't do it no 'ow.'

no ways. not in the least: 'I don't keer (care) no ways.'

nob, nobble. see **nab.**

nobbling stick, knocknobbler, sluggard-waker. a stick used in church by the clerk to wake sleeping people in the congregation.

nobbut. nothing but, only.

nockerlate. to vaccinate.

noddy. a noodle.

none the more. none the less.

noo. new.

noodlin'. behaving aimlessly.

noot, nowt, noothink. nothing. **noothink extry,** not well in health.

nor. than.

nose-warmer. a short-stemmed clay pipe.

nut. head: 'Off'n 'is nut,' out of his mind.

nuther. (pronounced like other), neither.

obedience. a bob or curtsey.

object. originally **abject,** a despised person, odd-looking, ugly, a figure of fun: 'I niver seed sech a old objec'.'

obleege. to oblige, to render service, to do a kindness. 2 to compel: 'We was 'bleeged t' work arly an' late.'

obstropolus. obstreperous.

ock'ard. see **awk'ard.**

odds. difference: 'What you think don't make no odds ter me.' 2 concern: 'Taint no odds o' yourn.'

odd-come-shorts. odds and ends.

oddydod, oddendod, oddysnail. snail. See **hoddod.**

o-er, ower. over.

of, o'. of. 2 from: 'Come out o'ther.' 3 on: 'We mostly goos of a Sunday.' 4 a superfluous preposition: 'I was but a-doin' of my dooty.'

off. off. **off'n, off of,** from: 'Git a loaf off of the baker.'

offish. stand-off: 'Sims a bit offish today, dunt 'e?'

o-geeing. tasking of the leading horse (Whoa – gee-up) in the harvest field from shock to shock of corn. See **horse cries.**

ol'as. see **al'ays.**

old Dobyn's path. accustomed ways: 'Hertfordshire country men scorn to be put out of their old Dobyn's path, as believing no way so good as their own.' (Ellis)

old-fashioned. cunning, knowing: 'he looked at her old-fashioned.'

old ones. parent birds or animals.

ommick, yommick. to trample about doing damage.

on. of: 'the both on 'em.' 'The fust I've 'eard on 't.' 2 as a prefix in the place of un: oncommon, onnat'ral.

once in a day. seldom, now and then.

oncommon. very.

onsensible. mad.

on'y. only. 2 but, excepting.

ook, oo-ak, ooken. oak: 'A grene ook.' (Chaucer)

'ooman. woman.

oon, woon. one: ... 'the oon was deed' (dead). (Chaucer)

oorchard. orchard, see also **archard**.

oosen. whose.

oots, oo-ats, wuts. oats.

ope. open: 'Wull'e ope th' gate fer me?'

or ever. before: 'Or ever the silver cord be loosed.'

ornary. ordinary.

orts. remnants, scraps of food, etc.

oshey (ozhey), also **ashlin.** soft ground fit for growing osier.

ought. should: 'Ye ough'ter do it.' **oughtn't,** shouldn't.

ourn, ou-ern. our (our one), ours.

ourself. ourselves.

out. away.

outn. out of: 'Adam an' Eve was druv outn th' gardin o' Eden, an'
the giate was shet on 'em. All the work as they ed done wus
gorn fer nowt. An' as Adam went a-proggin' on, fair mazed an'
mizzle-mozzled in 'is 'ead, an' luggin' little Cain an' Abel be the
'and, ther sprung up all around 'em the fust thistles an' docks
an' nittles an' burrs as iver was.'

out'n-outer. one who goes farther than others.

over-done it. overslept.

overlook. to shadow, bewitch.

overtook. mistaken.

over-thirtin'. cross ploughing land already ploughed.

overthrow. to upset, turn over.
> 'Well plowed, well mowed,
> And ne'er a load overthrowed.'
>   (Mow and throw rhyme with plow in Herts.)

ov'n. ovens were of brick and were heated with faggots or gorse
sticks. The ashes were swept out with the mawker and the
unbaked loaves slipped in on the peel.

owlet. 'As poor as an owlet.' (Old saying.)

owl's light. dusk.

owt. anything: 'Be ther any noos (news) o'owt?' 'Nay, nowt.

P

pace. step: 'It aint more'n a two-three paces t' th' Church.'

pack. to be sent away hurriedly: 'Ye desarve to be sent packin'.'

packman. pedlar.

pad. a saddle horse.

paddin'. to come or go on foot: 'The lion came a great padding pace.' (*Pilgrim's Progress*)

paddy. a temper: 'she's in a paddy.'

padway. space between ruts in a road.

paigle, peggle, cow-peggle. cowslip. **peggle-peeps** (pips), petals of cowslip, used to make cowslip wine. Isaac Walton liked cowslip pips fried with trout.

palfrey. horse for the road.

pan. hard surface of clay, subsoil.

parcel, pa'cel. a number or quantity, large or small, of anything:
'What's that n'ise I 'ear?'
'Jist a pa'cel o' silly gals a-screechin'.'

parky. cold.

parlour. a downstairs bedroom. **bes' parlour,** sitting room.

pask-flower. anemone.

pat. opportunely, perfectly. **off pat,** well learned.

pa'tridge. partridge. Pa'tridge was correct 17th century pronunciation.

pattens, pattings. wooden soles mounted on iron rings strapped to the feet for use in wet weather.

pay on or **out.** to take revenge: 'I'll pay 'im out ... e'll git as good as 'e gon (gave)'.

peaky. of delicate, wan appearance.

peale. scolding. See **rogue.**

pecker. small pick-axe for cutting furze.

peckish. hungry.

peek. to peep.

peel. a long-handled wooden shovel used to put unbaked loaves into the brick ovens.

peg. to wedge, fasten. 2 to walk or work with determination and perseverance: "'e come peggin' up the road like a youngster, an 'im in 'is eighty-four.'

pelt. the skin of a beast. 2 to run fast: 'The bull coom peltin' a'ter me.' 3 to pour down: 'A peltin' rain.' 'They were all in a pelting heat.' (*Pilgrim's Progress*)

performance. happening, story: 'I'll tell 'e th' 'ole performance.'

perish. to die; to **perish himself,** to commit suicide: 'One Wilshere perished himself.' (*History of Hitchin*)

perishin', perishy. bitterly cold: 'A perishin' wind.'

perk. to prink: 'Perkin' at 'erself in the glass.'

perky. lively, trim, self-satisfied. 2 forward, early (of wheat, etc.).

perty. pretty. 2 nicely: 'The lil gal said 'er bit wery perty.'

pert 'nigh, pri'-nigh. nearly.

pested. over-run: 'Pested with rats an' meece.'

pest'us. originally a house for isolating small-pox patients. At the time of the Great Plague, the Mayor of St. Albans opened a pest-house in the Hatfield road for the unhappy people who, in spite of his ministration, were dying in the streets. As a rule, people who had plague were isolated in their own houses and were buried in their backyards. 'Edward Barker, Elizabeth his wife and Ellen his daughter were buried on their own backside at Two Waters, dying of the plague.'

pharisees. properly fairieses: fairies.

pickid. pointed, sharp.

pickle. child (affectionate).

pictur'. anyone or anything pretty: 'She's a pictur' an no mistake'.

piece. a term of contempt, applied to a woman. 2 a gun: "is old fowlin' piece 'anged o'er the chimbley-shelf.'

pigsie, pigsney. (pig's eye), a term of affection towards girl children: 'Miss, mine own Pigsnie...' (Sir Philip Sidney)

pig-slap or **slat.** a wooden bat used by pig-drovers.

pightle, pikle. an enclosure adjoining a farmhouse in which cattle were kept at night. The pightle is now usually an orchard.

pike. to pry, be nosy; to pike about, to nose around.

piker, pikey. a tramp.

pilch. a triangular flannel worn by babies.

pimble, pingle. to eat fastidiously, picking over food: 'She eats nex' ter nuffin' ... jist pimbles er meat (food), a peck 'ere an' there an' that's all.'

pimmick. a fanciful person: ''er's a p'or pimmick ... a-pimblin' 'er figgy-duff to 'ocks the tit-bits. I tell 'er she'll come to want one of these days an then she'll be sorry.'

pimp. small bundle of cut wood for fire lighting.

pimping machine. for cutting wood, also used in Sussex.

pinch. an emergency, the last resort.

pinchers. pincers.

pipe. to whistle. 2 **to take a pipe,** to smoke: 'After supper as he sat by the Fyre, he took a pipe of Tobacco.' **pipin-'ot, 'ot as 'ot,** as hot as can be, sizzling.

pis-n. poison.

pissums, pismires. ants. **pissums' nestes,** also pissums' banks, ant-hills or heaps and anty-tumps.

pitch. stature, height or depth. 2 a steep part of a road: 'Nip out o'th' cart an' walk up this pitch'. 3 to throw, lift. 4 to pave or face with stones.

pitcher. man who pitches hay on to haycart or rick with a pitchfork. 2 see **games**.

pitchin. a cobble-paved yard.

pitchins. (see **pitch**), rounded flint pebbles or cobbles, largely used in Hertfordshire for paving yards and paths. These were found in river-gravels and came originally from the chalk.

pith. strength.

placket. the opening in skirt or petticoat; originally placket was a petticoat.

plague. nuisance: 'They flies is a plague!'

plain. any level land.

plaishin' or **plashin' and dubbin'.** see **hedge**.

plash, also **wash.** a small pool.

a plenty. many, a good crop.

plosh. splash: 'Ploshing through the durt over my shoes, having no pattings on.' (Hine, *History of Hitchin*)

plough. The great Hertfordshire plough was of wood, and was drawn by 8 oxen yoked to a pole, 16 ft 6 ins. long (the pole or perch measurement).

In a 4-horse team the horses were called for'ost (foremost), secon' for'ost, body-'oss and thiller.

plow. to plough. Hertfordshire made a difference between the noun and the verb in spelling the word.

plum bobs. raisins tied in a piece of linen, given to a baby as a pacifier (also used in Tudor times).

plum-pudding stone. conglomerate, consisting of glacial gravel, local and far-travelled pebbles and stones, cemented by calcium-carbonate. See the great block at Willbury Park. (Hine, *National History of Hitchin district*)

poliwogs. frog-tadpoles. Tadpole proper is a young toad.

poll. head: 'ev 'e boomped 'is po'r poley, then?' (to a child).

pollards. meal, in quality between dan and bran.

poodlin'. hobbling: 'e come a-poodlin' a'ter us, 'ollerin' at th' top o' 'is v'ice' (voice).

pood'n-fut. club foot.

poorlings. children dependent on the parish.

pop. to go or come suddenly. 2 to smack a child in the proper place.

poppet. young child (affectionate).

po'r. poor.

po'r 'us. workhouse, now institution.

porch. to poach. **porcher, pocher,** a poacher: There were porchers and 'common porchers, not qualyfyed to keep neither dogs, nor netts, nor gunns, nor no such thing.' (Herts Sessions Rolls, 1693)

'As I and my compani-ons,
Was settin' of a sna-er,
The keeper was a-watchin' us,
For 'im we did not ca-er
For we can wrastle and fight, me boys,
And pop out any wheer,
And it's my delight
Of a shiny night,
In the season of the year.' (Old song)

post, poust. (plural, es): 'The ow'd postes ev bin perished this long

whoile.' 'We'd best ev a noo fence o'pousts an' rials (rails)'.
''ark 'e! I seed three magpoys a-settin' on three poustes.' 'Ye
dunt s'y so! An' 'ow many arf a pints 'ad ye 'ad?'

pot herbs. mixed vegetables for a stew.

pour, downpour. heavy rain.

a power of. a great deal: ''e ad a mint o'money an' 'e done (did) a
power o' good w'th it.'

powldered. powered, crushed.

powny, poany. pony.

pray. a common expression of surprise: 'O pray! I niver could a
bleeved it on 'im!' 2 a superfluous expression at the end of a
sentence: ''Oo may you be, pray? An' 'ow long ev yer bin 'ere?'

precious, also **mighty**: 'A precious lot o' good.' 'A mighty shiame'
(shame).

prig. to filch, steal:
        ''im as prigs what isn't 'isn,
        When 'e's cotched 'll goo t' prison.' (Old saying.)

prim-e-rose. primrose:
        'Eke eche at other threw the floures bright,
        The primerose, the violete, and the gold.'

prim-e-rose-time. early Spring.

proper. thorough, thoroughly.

proud flesh. new skin around a wound.

pry. to look closely.

puddle. (short u), puddle. 2 to paddle, to make dirty: 'Sech a leetle
muck ye niver seed! Puddlin' in the pond up ter 'is knees in slud
(mud)'.

puddock. a frog.

puggy. muggy, damp, sticky. 2 common name for a ferret: 'When
the ferret came from the hole we gave it the back of our hand to
sniff at, saying Puggy, Puggy, come along, Puggy, until it was far
enough out of the hole to be picked up.'

pull. to pluck.

pully-hauly. pull together: 'Are ye ready? Then pul-ly-hauly.'

pun. pound (singular and plural): 'A ten-pun note! Well, that's
better ner a smack on the 'ead, if they 'it iver ser 'ard.'

purpis. purpose: ''Twarn't a accident, I tell 'e, 'e done it a-purpis.'

purrock. paddock.

push. a boil, gathering.

put about. inconvenienced, upset.

'put the miller's eye out'. add too much liquid to flour etc in cooking.

put-to. to harness.

quag. quagmire: 'Behold on the left hand was a very dangerous quag.' (*Pilgrim's Progress*)

quamp. to squash, subdue: 'I'll quamp 'em, the yong mischiefs.'

quare, queer. ill in body or mind. 2 odd, unconventional: ''e's a quare 'un an' no mistake.'

quarter. to drive a carriage or cart between ruts (see **ruts**).

quick. usually hawthorn.

quick-hedge, quick-set-hedge. hedge made chiefly of hawthorn.

quiff. whiff. 2 knack: 'Once ye git the quiff on't it's easy enough.' 3 a strange or amusing thing.

quirky. nervous.

qu't. pronunciation of cwt., a hundredweight, heard as recently as 1941 at Watford.

rabbit you. 'confound you'. See **drabbit**.

rack, rag, scrag. neck of mutton. 2 **rack up,** to tend farm-horses and prepare stable for the night.

rakes. ruts: 'Paid to a shovell man for two days to shovell in the cart rakes.' (Herts Sessions Rolls, 1672)

ramps. romps, noisy movements.

rare. excellent.

rassel. 'out on the rassel', have a good time.

rastling. wrestling.

rathe. early flowering or ripening.

rather, ruther. sooner, more willingly: 'Rather a booket (bucket) o' swill ner (than) a boonch o' roses, sez th' owd sow.'

rattle. a talkative person. 2 noisy, empty talk: ''e kip rattlin' on, blowin' 'is own trompet: 'e wants th' arth, siminly, but 'e'll find 'isself on a dung'll w'th 'is comb cut.'

ravished. hungry.

rawk, rowk. to rake, stir up.

rawky. raw (of weather), bitter cold.

reap, rip. to reap: 'Workin' on the land is wuth-while work. In me time I worked fo-urteen an' fifteen 'ow-ers a day. We use ter sow be 'and and rip be 'and throsh wuth th' ol' frail (flail). Sometimes we'd ev ter dibble the seed in, an' sometimes we sowed 'en broadcast. At 'arvis' time we cut wuth a sickle: we tuk a' an'ful o'carn an' lef' a fut o'haulm (stalk) standin', so then the sheaves waant ser big. We use ter cut beans wuth a sickle or a 'ook, an' baarley was mowed wuth a scythe an' carried loose inter th' barn.'

reasy, reasty. rancid, usually bacon, butter or dripping.

rec'lec'. to recollect.

reefin', reekin'. smoking: 'It hong (hung) in the chimbley, a-reefin' over night.' **reeky, reechy,** smoky.

reglar. complete: 'a reg'lar fix.'

rench. to rinse.

reve. to rob, snatch, tear: "e'd a riv (reved) the shirt off'n me back ef I'd let 'im.' **reeve,** steward.

ribbin, riband. ribbon: 'A boonch o' blue ribbins.'

rick, reck. see **stack**.

rid. rode.

ridder. a sieve. **riddle,** to sift.

rightly. exactly, truly.

rile. to annoy.

rin. ran, run.

ripe. to ripen: 'The time of the year when black cherries begin to ripe.' (Herts Sessions Rolls, 1703)

rise. slope: 'Now for a canter up the rise.'

road, roadway. usually the high road. **any road,** anyway, in any case: 'Any road, I'll see for myself.'

rogue. 'An old rogue and a rascal.'

rong. rung of a ladder.

rookin'. wandering aimlessly.

rootlin', routlin'. turning up the ground. 2 **rout,** to bring out after a search.

rose. risen.

rough music. a discordant serenade with banging of kettles and trays, clanging of bells, before the house of newly-wedded people, the performers hoping for 'larges' or beer. 2 A noisy protest under the window of an immoral couple.

rough weather. wet and miserable.

round-frock. see **smock**.

rowen. second crop of hay. 2 stubble left unploughed.

rowl. to roll: 'The Flood came down, rowling like the Bay of Biscay …' (Letter to Sir Hans Sloane on the great hailstorm at Hitchin, May 4th, 1697.)

rowst, rost. to scold: 'She dint 'alf rowst 'er ol' man.'

rub. difficulty.

rubber. whetstone for scythes of hard white grit, carried by mowers in a leather pouch.

rubbige. rubbish.

ruinated. ruined: 'A very poor woman ... very much dampnified and ruinated.' (Herts Sessions Rolls, 1681)

rum. strange, queer: 'That's a rum goo howsiver.'

rumble. to understand, or see through deception: 'I rumbled 'im'.

rum'un. an eccentric person.

run up. to build or make anything quickly.

runty. ill-tempered. 2 poor, skinny.

ruts, to take the ruts. to keep the wagon-wheels in the ruts. **to quarter the ruts,** to drive a carriage or cart between them.

ruttle, also **crickle.** to break up, crumble (of earth). 2 to press down: 'See ere, boy, that aint a barrerful o' kindlin' (firewood) ... Ruttle it down a bit an' it'll 'old a 'arf as mooch agin.'

Outside the mill at Wheathampstead; Mr James Titmuss, Mr Alf Freeman, Mr Rozier and Mr Bygrave. When taking the cart down rough country roads, the driver would take the ruts. (Mrs Amy Coburn)

saace. impertinence. **sa-acy,** impudent.

sad. of weather, mizzling or wet: 'A sad morning!' 'Sad weather for the harvest.' 2 heavy bread or cake.

sadly. in poor heath.

safe. certain.

saggy. wilting.

salery. celery.

sallow, sollar, sally. willow:
> 'Be the oak ne'er so stout,
> The sollar red will wear it out.' (Herts saying)

Sarad'y. Saturday: 'The sun al'ays shines a Saradays.' (Old saying)

sarch. search.

saun'in', sauntering.

save your bacon. to be just in time.

sawny. foolish, a foolish fellow.

say. tell: 'Say 'im 'e's wanted.' 2 **I say,** used at the beginning of a sentence, to call attention. **sayin', as the sayin' is,** commonly used at the end of a sentence, usually irrelevantly: 'They might, as the saying is, hear your horse dash.' (*Pilgrim's Progress*)

saye. silk.

scand'lous. reprehensible.

scant. scanty. 2 (of a horse) to grip the road with the hoofs going downhill.

scarecrow. The chief scarecrow was the **hodmidod,** which wore a hat and carried a stick for a gun. Others were the **boggard, bogle** (goblin), **mammet, maulkin,** and the **shewell,** a poor thing without hat or gun.

scares, skeers. fears: 'The Lord was pleased to keep scares out of my heart.' (Hine, *Hitchin Worthies*)

scart. scared.

scavenger. road-cleaner.

scholard. any educated person.

schoolin'. education.

scidders. scissors. 2 a cutting glance: 'The gal looked scidders at me.'

scotch. brake to prevent a wheel from turning.

scould. scold: 'Charged for being a common scould and peace-breaker.' (Herts Sessions Rolls, 1697)

scour. to clear and clean a ditch.

scrabble, scrobble. scramble.

scrats. pork fat scraps.

scronch. scrunch. Cottagers used to give their pigs a handful of cinders or small coal 'to scronch and to keep 'em busy.'

scrooge, scrowge. to huddle together.

scrounge. to slack, scamp work. 2 to cadge.

scrub. a stunted or insignificant person: 'A sorry scrub.' (*Pilgrim's Progress*)

scrummage (see **skarmish**), **scrummagin'.** routing about.

scrump. to steal fruit, usually apples, from the tree: 'I warrant they boys are fer scrumpin' me apples.'

scrumpt. dried up: 'The seedlin's was all scrumpt for want o' a drop o' waater.'

scrush. to crush, squeeze. **scruse, scrose,** crushed, squeezed: 'I never could abear ter be scrose.'

scurrocks. fragments, clippings of stuff.

seam. lard, hog fat.

see, seen, seed, sin. saw, seen: 'ev any on yer seed me little boy?' 'I sin 'im on'y a min'te agoo.' 'I see 'im gooin' oop street.'

see'ere. attend to what I am saying. **seein' as 'ow,** seeing that.

seed, sid. seed. **seed-lip, sid-cut,** bag for seed or shaped wooden box hooked on a leather belt and worn by husbandmen when broadcasting seed. 'Sow seeds by the new moon.' 'Never sow seeds by a waning moon.' (Herts sayings)

seep. an oozing up or away of water.

seldom. fairly often: 'Does this stream dry up in summer?' 'Not wery seldom it don't' (not very often).

sen. since: 'I aint sin (seen) 'im sen Saraday.'

sennight. seven nights, a week.

sense. reason. **no sense,** in no way: 'I tried me best but I cou'nt do ut no sense.'

sere. withered: 'Squire lets us gether the sere wood.'

ser'ous. serious, glum: 'Lor' bless my 'eart, ye nee'nt look ser serious! 't aint as bad as all that!'

servants in husbandry. see **husbandmen.**

set. to sit. 2 to plant:
> 'Sow dry,
> Set wet.' (Old saying)

set eyes on, also **clap eyes on.** to see: 'I aint set eyes on 'im sen Chirs'mas.'

set up. to stable: 'When they had set up their horses …'

shack, also **horrocks.** litter of broken straw, etc., left after a rick is cleared away: ''ere, we'd best clear up thisyer shack afore we goo.' 2 grain fallen from ripe ears, beech mast, etc., eaten by hogs after harvest.

shackles. stew, poor without meat.

sharp. to sharpen.

sharps, sharts, also **thill.** shafts of a cart.

shatterags. tatters: 'Coom on out o'they bushes: yer clo'es'll be tore ter shatterags.'

shaven-pate. see **joult-skull.**

shay. chaise: 'The powny-shay 'ud be the better fer a lick o' paint.'

she. her: 'I shou'nt like t' be seen along o'she.'

sheafs. sheaves.

sheckles. iron fastenings of hurdles.

sheen. machine.

shere, sheer. shire: ''arfordsheer's our Country.'

shet. to shut. **shetters,** shutters.

shewell. see **scarecrow.**

shift. to move: 'Oh pray don' shif' me, me ribs is bruk or summut.' 'Shift that cart out o' the road.' 2 to move away: 'We'll be shiftin' 'ouse come Lady Day.' 3 a woman's chemise. 4 to eat greedily: ''e did shift a goodish lot.' 5 to accomplish with an effort: 'They made a pretty good shift to wag along.' 'They looked well to their steps, and made a shift to get staggering over.' (*Pilgrim's Progress*) 6 to manage somehow.

ship. sheep. **ships' cla-as** (claws), **ships' fit** (feet), trotters.

shit, shet. shut, bolted: ''er shet the dooer in me fiace (face).' **to get shit/shot of,** to get rid: 'Ye'd bes' git shit o' th' lot.'

shiver. fragments. **shivereens, smithereens,** small fragments.

shock, also **stook.** a group of 5-10 corn sheaves standing together.

shockin'. bad, disgraceful: 'A shockin' cough.'

shoe. boot. **shoon,** boots.

shoot. to do something quickly: 'When I 'eard 'em cry *fi-er*, I shot out o' me bed an' inter me clo'es an' was out o' th' ouse in a twinkle.'

shore up. to prop up.

shot. also **av akker** (acre), half-acre. Shot was originally a nook, corner or butt, later a portion of tillage a furlong in length. The word is found in place names which were used in remote times, before monastic ownership of land. 2 an attempt. 3 a measurement of distance: **a bow-shot,** originally a bow-shoot.

shou'nt. should not.

shouting. part of a ceremonious welcome: 'He called to a trumpeter to entertain Christian with shouting and sound of trumpet for joy.' (*Pilgrim's Progress*)

shovel-men. road-menders: 'Laid out by Thomas Bird surveyor of the upland, for the mending of the highways: given to the shovel men to drinke to encourage them, £0 01 6. Given them more in the highway to encourage them to work harder £0 0 6.' (Herts Session Rolls, 1672)

showl. shovel:
'Who'll dig his grave?
I, said the owl,
With my spade and showl.'

shrewd. dangerous, ill-natured.

shrimp. a small person or child.

shuck. to shell peas. Shucks were the peapods.

shuff. shy.

shut in. to harness. **shut out,** to unharness.

shut knife. pocket knife.

shy. to fight shy of: "'e fit (fought) shy o' th' gal thrickly (directly) 'e seed as she was a'ter 'im.'

sich, sich-like, sech. such.

sickle. The sickle was used for reaping when the straw was to be cut halfway up. This haulm was mown with the scythe after harvest and used for litter or for laying on the roofs of small sheds or hovels.

sid, sidcut, sidlip. see **seed**.

sidehill. hillside.

sight. many, much: 'A good sight more 'taters.' 2 a figure of fun (also **sketch**).

sin. seen: 'Waal, Muster Webb, oi be pleased to a sin yer again.' 2 since.

sink. to fail (in illness). 2 to dig a well. **sink away,** a porous drain.

sit, set. to sit: 'Coom in an' sit ye down,' a common welcome.

sitty hen. broody hen.

sixt. sixth.

skarmish, also **scrimmage, scrummage.** skirmish, brawl.

skedaddle. to be sent off or to leave hurriedly.

skeg. sloe.

sketch. see **sight**.

skew-wise. not straight.

skew your eye. to look along a line: 'Skew your eye along the thurrer (furrow) … whoy! it's as crooked as a dog's 'ind leg.'

skoshes. grains of corn which slip, still in husk, through the threshing-machine.

slabbin. thick slabs, sawn from elm butts and used for the walls of pig-sties.

slabby. muddy. See **slud**.

slap. well: 'That aint done very slap.' **slap-dabbin' about,** messing about.

slatter. scatter.

slave-sack. an empty sack put on a man's back under a full one. 2 the lowest sack of a pile.

sleep them. to find beds: "'owiver kin I sleep 'em all?'

slep. slept.

slick. immediately. 2 artful.

slip through the hedge. to die: 'So the ol' lady's gorn at last! What time did she slip through the hedge?' (This old expression was heard in 1942 in E. Herts.)

slipe, slip. a narrow strip of agricultural land. 2 a slip of wood. 3 spinney. The word occurs in places names: Slipe Farm, Slip End. 4 slender: 'a slip of a girl.'

slippy. quickly. 2 slippery.

slither. to slide, slip. **slithery, sliddery,** slippery.

sliver. a small slice or piece. 2 a hard blow or cut: 'I cotched 'im a sliver on the ja-a (jaw), that I did.' 3 to divide.

slocker. a quiet walk.

slommuck, slummock. slattern. 2 to treat things carelessly.

slop. (originally a sort of breeches), a light-coloured cotton coat.

slud. thick, foul mud, slush. **sluddy,** muddy.

sluggard-waker. see **nobbling stick.**

sluggy. sluggish.

smert. smart, clever, brisk.

smirk. neat, trim. 2 to smile affectedly: ''er'll smirk at 'ersen (herself) in the glass be the 'ou-er t'gither.'

smirry. of weather, damp, drizzling.

smitch. knob on the wick of a candle. 2 to snuff: 'Jist smitch the dip, wull 'e?'

smith. this was the work of the village smith: 'to shoe cart-horse, carriage-horse, nag, cob, pony and ass; to weld and fix tires of tumbrills and wagons; to sharpen coulters, blades, teeth of ploughs, scarifiers and harrows; to attend to the clappers of bells; to solder and mend, ring pigs and apply the best tallow to soothe pain, to saw off the tusks of any destructive boar.'

smitten. taken with, like.

smock or **round-frock.** a loose linen garment, the common outer wear of husbandmen. It was gathered (smocked) over the chest and back and was usually made of dark green linen for workadays and of white linen for Sundays, this being sometimes embellished with stitched patterns and small blue beads. For churchgoing the smock was worn with a black or grey top hat.

s'mo-er. some more.

The Smithy at Ayot St Peter: 'to shoe carthorse, carriage-horse, nag, cob, pony and ass...' (Mrs Amy Coburn)

smoke-penny. a tax of a penny or less on each hearth, collected from Saxon times on St Peter's day and sent to support the English College in Rome.

smooth. to fondle, stroke.

smouldry, smothery. suffocating.

smut. also called a black (see **thief**).

snail. Hertfordshire still has the great 'Roman snail' (probably brought earlier from Gaul) which like the native snail, was valued as a remedy for consumption. It was eaten raw and said by connoisseurs to equal the oyster in flavour.

snatch. snack: 'I got a pint o'beer an' a snatch o' grub at the Red Lion.' 2 a mouthful of hay or grass: 'Th' 'osses 'ull git a snatch o'grass be the roadside.'

sneak. to steal, pilfer. 2 tell tales.

sned. the curved stale (handle) of a scythe.

snob. cobbler, to cobble: 'I're gooin' 'ome arly ter do a bit o'snobbin'.'

sno-er. snore: 'Be th' way ol' Granfaa's a-snoerin', 'e mun be 'evin a rare job t' git 'is pigs ter markit.'

snotty. horrid, poor: 'A snotty ol' gardin (garden).'

snottygobbles. yew berries.

snow in 'arvist. a long face, 'cheerful as snow in 'arvist.'

snully. crooked: 'The snully-'orned 'eifer.'

snupsole. grappling iron for getting things out of wells.

sock. a blow.

sockly. slovenly.

softy-sawny. soft-headed.

soggy, suggy. (of soil), wet, unworkable.

so-ho. cry on sighting a hare when coursing. 2 used as a greeting: 'So-ho, friend, let us have your company.' (*Pilgrim's Progress*) 3 cry of horseman on entering an inn-yard.

soldier. stickleback. See **stittlebat**.

soo-ut. suet.

soppy. very wet, soppin'-wet.

sore, so-er. sore, trouble: 'Well you know your sore and I know mine.' (*Pilgrim's Progress*)

sort of. kind. 2 what o'clock: 'What sort o' time is it?'

sot. a drunkard. 2 sat: 'I sot meself down on th' long form be th' fier an' Obby Day coom an' sot aside o'me, an' t'other chaps coom an' sotted therself down, an' we ed a glass o' beer, an' we was wery coomfable t'gither.'

sour. disagreeable: 'She's es sour es a green apple.'

sowbugs. woodlice.

sowl. soul.

spake. to speak: 'Not much to spake on (of)'.

spalt. split.

sparagras. asparagus.

spar'awk. sparrow-hawk.

spare. to omit. 2 to take no trouble: 'Ye'll niver be no good if ye spares y'rself o-er yer job. 'ev'n't ye iver 'eard:
    'Idle folk as takes no trouble,
    Al'ays make ther labour double.' (Old saying.)

sparin'. thrifty, saving.

sparrer, spadger, joey-spadger. sparrow. **'edge-pooper,** hedge sparrow.

spat. spot: 'a spat o'rain.'

spell. magic, still in use as a threat: 'I'll put a spell on yer, see ef I dunt.'

spence. a basket of plaited rushes used by husbandmen and carters for carrying food. Also called **howlet** about Hinxworth.

spendthrift. a doubtful or bad character. 2 a poacher.

spet. to spit. **spetted,** spat.

spewy, spewiness. damp, ozziness (of soil).

spike. a dwarf spire. 'Hertfordshire spikes' are found on a number of churches.

spile, spiol. spoil.

spin out. to use sparingly.

spirtle, spurtle. to spirt or sprinkle: 'It spirtles o'rain.' 'I'll spirtle some water over the flowers to freshen them.'

spit. an accumulation of gravel or sand in a stream.

splatter. to spatter.

splay-fut. splayfoot.

splificate. to stifle.

splodge. to splash.

splotch. a spot, blot, dab of dirt, etc.

sprak. quick and lively, clean and neat.

spreathed. chapped, sore legs.

sprindle. an implement used in thatching.

spring, also **coupiss.** coppice. Hertfordshire was at one time noted for its 'coupisses'. 2 a well or source.

sprinkle. scatter.

spruce. to get tidy: 'Ye med as well spruce oop a bit.'

spur up. to support. A gatepost, broken near the ground, is spurred up by a piece of wood set in the ground alongside and nailed above the break.

spurway. bridle path.

spy. a look: 'Le's (let us) ev a spy at 'em.'

squab. to fall down.

squabby, squaddy. fat.

squad. thick mud.

squag. to shake up.

squandered. scattered: 'Parson's a bit too old for such a squandered parish.'

squashy. a wet patch in a meadow.

squench. to quench.

squiggle, scriggle. to wriggle.

squine, squeen. to whine, to make a fretful sound. A horse squines when the girths are tightened.

stack. a rick: a stack was usually of corn, a rick of hay, but either word was used.

staddle. prop, staff, foundation. 2 a frame to raise ricks from the ground, laid upon upright stones about 2 ft. high.

stag. see **hedge**.

stale, stayl. the shaft or handle of a tool or implement.

stank. a dam. 2 to lay boards, supported by piles or struts, at the sides and bends of watercourses to strengthen the banks.

stare. to show astonishment: 'It 'ould a med (have made) yer stare.'

start. happening: 'That's a quare start.' 2 a fright: 'It give me a start.'

statty. the Statute Fair at which men and maids were hired.

staver, stapole, stang. post, pillar, stake or staple. 2 boundary marks.

stayers. stairs.

stead. place.

steed. horse, originally a battle-horse.

stew. fuss.

stiddy. steadily: 'I'll be gittin' stiddy back 'ome now.'

stile. a set of steps by which to pass from field to field.

stingy. bitter: 'A stingy east wind.' **stinger,** a hard blow.

stint. limit. 2 allotted amount of work.

stitch. distance: 'You have gone a good stitch, you may well be weary.' (*Pilgrim's Progress*)

stittlebat, tittlebat, tiddler, also **bam, soldier.** stickleback. In Spring, when the male is tinged with red, it is also called Fiery King.

stock, stocks. sawn timber, logs. 2 brickwork at the back of a gate.

stockwood, stockings. land cleared of timber.

stolch. to walk through mud or slush.

stomp. stamp, stumped.

stond. stood.

stone-pickers. small gangs of children who gathered stones on arable land under the direction of their foreman, a boy of ten or eleven years: 'Take yer pails. Pick the stones up clean. Chuck'em out o' the pail on ter th' 'eap. The cart'll take 'em away.' The stones were used for road-mending.

stool. stole.

stoop. to tilt: 'Stoop your eend (end) up a bit mer (more)'.

stout it out. to brazen out.

straight, striaght. truly: 'I will do it for you, I will, straight. You can trust me.'

stride. to measure by pacing: 'I know 'ow fur t'is, I strid it meself.'

strike, also **hit.** to come to, hit off: 'Keep on and you'll strike the high road.' 'The stream flows down till it strikes the river near the mill.' 2 to keep a straight course to a given point: 'Strike across the downs till you hit the old drovers' road.' 3 level off corn in measure.

strip. a portion of land, from half to 3 or 4 acres, in the great open arable fields; a man could hold several strips in different parts of the field.

strow. to strew. **strown, straad,** strewn.

struck on. to admire, like: 'I aint mooch strook on th' noo gal.'

stub. the stump of a tree. 2 to knock the foot against anything. **to stub up,** to dig out stumps, roots, etc.

stub rabbit. young bucks turned out of the warren by their jealous elders.

stulches. layers of straw of the width of a man's armreach, and laid on a roof by the thatcher.

stump. a short walk: 'Let's go for a stump between the showers.'

stun'. stone (singular and plural): 'It weighs ten stun' five pun.'

stunner. anything large or of good quality. 2 one who does kind and charitable deeds.

sturrup. stirrup, formerly called irons.

sub. an advance of wages.

suckers. lollipops, sweets.

suddent. sudden.

sukey. a kettle.

summin'. arithmetic.

summut. somewhat. **summut, soonthin',** something: ''e gon (gave) me a summut an' whatcher think it wer? Twas a goold suvrin.'

sun'. sound: 'I n'er 'eard a sun' on't.'

sun-stone. also called God-stone, a waterworn transparent pebble often carried for luck.

super, sooper. extra good or grand.

sure as 'arvis'. certain.

suspicious. to be suspected: 'Charles Rolfe is a very suspicious person ... and belongs to a gang of rogues.', (Herts Sessions Rolls, 1698)

swaarm. swarm, crowd.

swab. to shake, joggle: ''owd (hold) the ladder, wull 'e, so 's it dunt give. Th' ol' dog swabbed it jist now an' pert' nigh brung me down, ladder 'n all.'

swaed. also **swarth,** sward. **a bit o' swaed,** a sod of turf: 'We mun (must) stop oop them wapses nestes wuth a bit o'swaed.'

swaller. swallow. 2 a hole in the ground for water to run away. 3 to believe an unlikely story.

swarve. to swerve.

swell. a rise in the ground.

swelled. swollen.

swimmer. a floating dumpling, plain and eaten with jam or butter and sugar.

swimmy. giddy.

swinge. (soft g), the stroke of a flail, to strike: 'St George that swinged the dragon.' (Shakespeare, *King John*)

swipe, swiper. a hard slap: 'I fetched 'im a swiper.'

swipes. small beer.

swipper, swippy. nimble, agile.

swound. to swoon: 'I thought I sh'ud a swounded.'

swum. swam.

tachy. (pronounced tashy), of weather, spotting with rain.

tack. food of any kind.

tackle. gear for fastening, moving or holding: 'The tackle of my heart is cracked and burnt. (Shakespeare, *King John*). 2 harness. 3 to go at: 'I'll tackle yon job an' I'll git it done be night! Let them Irish scroungers what wanted three men put t' do it, see 'ow we work in 'arfordshere. I'll show 'em.' 4 threshing machine, run by the 'sheen men'.

tadpole. young toad: 'Some years th' tadpools 'atch out arlier than th' polywogs (young frogs), an' they eats the polywogs so as ther aint more'n a two-three frogs that season. But nes' (next) Spring, the polywogs coom out fust an' get a good start an' the y'ung to-ads 'as t' goo 'ungry or make do wuth wums an' sloogs.'

tail crop. second crop. See also **a'termath**.

take-off. an anonymous valentine, amusing or scurrilous.

take-on. to be angry, agitated or distressed.

take-up. to interrupt, contradict. **to take up the fire,** to put it out.

takin'. fuss, agitation: 'What a taking was he in.' (Shakespeare)

talk. to court, make love. **talkin',** courting: 'ev ye 'eard as your Tom an' our Liza's a-talkin' an' es bin this two month?' 'Aye, I knowed it. I met 'em oop th' twitchell (narrow lane) las' Soonday an' I sung 'em th' ol' song, an' neer split me sides a-laughin' t' see ther red faces.'
> 'A starry night for a ramble,
> Down in the flowery dell,
> An' a kiss behind a bramble,
> A kiss — and never tell.' (Old song)

tally-up. to count.

tan. to beat: 'I'll tan yer 'ide fer yer, ye lil deev'l.'

tanket. to tinker: 'Al'ways a-tankerin' at 'is ol' scythe.' 2 to follow, drive: 'Missus comes tanketin' a'ter me fro' morn t' night.' See also **hocksin'**.

tanstickers. see **lucifers.**

tantalise. to tease.

tar. also **het,** to urge, encourage a dog.

tarble. terrible. 2 very, great.

'taters. potatoes.

teart. tender to the touch.

techy. touchy: 'Dunt yer be s' techy, missus (wife)! I can't ope' me mouth but what y're ready t' joomp down me throoat.'

ted. in haymaking, to shake and spread new mown grass:
'Go, sirs, and away
To ted and make hay.' (Tusser)

tell tale tit. a sneak.

telled, telt, tolt. told.

tend. to attend, look after: 'A po'r widowman, livin' alone an' tendin' to isself.'

ter. to: 'Terday an' termorrer.'

than what. than: ''e's better off than what I be.'

thank'e, thenk'e. thank you.

that. so, very: 'I wer that tired!' 2 used redundantly: 'Can you do it?' 'That I can. Ye'll see threcly'.

then-a-days. in time past.

ther, theer, tha-er. there, their.

therself, thersen. themselves.

thetch. thatch: 'Thetch yer roof with stra-a throshed be the thrail (threshed by the flail), an' it'll last twenty year an' more: sheen (machine) throshed straa wunt stand more'n ten year.'

thetch. vetch.

they. those: 'keep out o'they nittles.'

thief. also **waster,** a burning black or smut on the wick of a candle: 'Shift that ther thief, wull 'e, afore it starts gutterin'.'

thill, till, fill. the shaft of a cart or wagon. **thill'oss, thiller, wheeler,** the horse in the shafts. **thill harness,** cart-harness. See also **sharps.**

think on. to remember. 2 think of.

this all and some. the short and long of a story.

Thatched cottages at Great Wymondley: 'Thetch yer roof with stra-a throshed be the thrail, an' it'll last twenty year an' more.'

this an' all. an' all is a superfluous expression: 'I can't do this an' all, try es I may.'

thisere, thish yer. this; themther, those; this'n, this one; that'n, that one. Thisere is not this here, but the old Saxon word *thesera*, this.

thizzle. thistle: 'Taint a bit o' good cuttin' thizzles till arter S'n John's day' (June 24th). (Old saying)

thorough. through: 'The coote (coat) was without seame, woven uppon thorowe and thorowe.' (Coverdale's *New Testament*)

thrail, threshel. see **flail.**

thrailer, throsser, also **barntasker.** thresher: 'A good thrailer's every bit as good as a throshin-'sheen (machine) an' gits the kernals out jest as clean.' Thrailers were paid sixpence a bushel for threshing wheat, barley and oats, and fourpence for beans. 'He that eareth (plows) shulde ear upon hope, and he that throszheth shulde throszh upon hope.' (Coverdale's *New Testament*)

threadled. threaded.

threcly. directly.

thumb-bit, thrumb-bit. also called **doorstep,** two slices of bread, one larger than the other, with a chunk of meat or bacon between. The smaller piece of bread, pressed by the thumb, held the meat steady while bits were cut off the chunk.

thumpin'. also **thun'rin',** large: 'A thoompin' big marrer.'

thun'er. thunder: 'You don't need to be frit of thun'erbolts an' lightnin' if you have house-leeks growin' on your roof.' This belief was shared by Sir Thomas More: 'A sure defensative against thunder.'

thurrer, thorrer. furrow.

thwack. a blow.

thwart. to bridge: 'We 'ull ev ter thwart the branch (stream)'

tice. old form of entice.

tiddler. stickleback. See **stittlebat.**

tiddling with rain. drizzling.

tiddy, tiddly. tiny: '...little tiddy Bartholomew boarpig.' (Shakespeare, *Henry IV*)

tiddly-bump. bump: 'Down 'e coom, tiddly-boomp.'

tidy. neat. 2 considerable quantity: 'A tidy few apples, a good crop'. 3 satisfactory: 'I call that a tidy job.' 4 of health: 'quite 'alf tidy', fairly well; 'on'y 'alf tidy', not very well.

tiff. squabble.

tiggle. to tickle. 2 to move slowly. **tigglin' about,** also **messin' about,** doing odd jobs, nothing in particular: 'What's 'e a-doin' now?' 'Noothin' mooch, jist tigglin' about.' **tigglin' along,** sauntering.

time. when: 'Time we lived Redbourn way.'

time and again. often: 'Look a-'ere, missus, you've axed me time an' agin t' leave me 'ome an' goo in ter the townd. 't aint not a bit o' use 'ere I wus born an' 'ere I ull bide. Goo away! 't aint likely my toime o' life, so jist you start t' think!'

ting-tang. the 5-minutes or sermon bell.

tinker. to mend after a fashion.

tip, tippit, tittip, tittup. to walk lightly, to patter. 2 to trot: 'The powny coom tippitin' oop the road.'

tipplin' 'ouse. alehouse. (Herts Sessions Rolls, 1621)

tit, tittle, tipple o-er. to tumble over, over-balance.

tit an' turn. any small trouble or difficulty.

titch. to touch.

to. at, these words are interchangeble, see **at.**

to an' froo. to and fro.

tob. to throw. See **lob**.

tobyman. highwayman.

todgy. short and fat.

toe-rag. naughty child; 'little toe rag'. Also used by farm workers to bind their feet.

togged out. see also **trimmed out,** to be dressed up.

toggery. finery.

tokened. engaged to be married.

tol'able. fairly well.

tong. tongue.

tong-bangin'. a scolding.

took, tuk. taken: 'How many steps have I took in vain.' (*Pilgrim's Progress*) 2 used redundantly: 'When 'e see the constable 'e tuk an' run.' **took bad,** taken ill.

toot. to pry, 2 to search for game.

top-full. brim-full: 'Their souls are topful of success.' (Shakespeare, *King John*).

top-up. to finish the top of a rick before thatching it.

topperm'st. highest.

toppin. foremost. 2 excellent.

toppins. fine bran.

topple. a tumble.

tore out. also **wore out,** worn out.

tormint. torment, nuisance.

to'rds, tow-ards. towards.

tossel. tassel.

tot. a small mug or measure. 2 to pour out. **tot up,** to add.

tother, the tother. the other (orginally that other).

a-totherside. opposite.

touch. a spasm.

toucher. almost: **a near toucher,** a narrow shave.

towl. to toll: 'I paid 'im fer towlin' o' the bell.'

towld, tow'd. told.

townd. town: 'To the astonishment of the townde.' (Journal of George Fox, 1655)

trace. a sign. 2 to track, follow a course: 'Tracing and walking to and fro.' (*Pilgrim's Progress*) 'Tracing of hares in the snow with a grayhound.' (Herts Sessions Rolls. This was a common form of poaching.)

tramplin', also **ommockin'.** walking here and there, usually doing damage.

transport. a convict condemned to be transported; male transports were conveyed from Hertford to the Hulks at Woolwich for one shilling a head; females to the *Æolus* or other ships 'lying in the Gallions'.

trapse. to tread heavily, trudge. 2 to trail about in an idle way.

treat. very well: 'Iverything went a treat.'

trimmed out. see **togged out.**

trot. an old dame, originally trat.

trouncin'. scolding. 2 beating.

trow. trough.

trustles. trestles.

tryce. to drag away. 2 quickly.

tuck, a-tuckin' 'em down. to eat greedily.

tumbril. wagon.

tu'n. to turn.

turk. child (affectionate chiding).

turn. time, occasion: 'I cyant do it this turn.' 2 shock. 3 bout (in illness): ''e ad a smartish turn las' week.'

tu'nup, turmut. turnip.

tussocks. rough pasture; anthills; lumps of grass found by the river. See **jussocks.**

a twel'month. a year.

twichel, twidgel, twithern, twibeen. a narrow lane or passage.

twig. to observe, detect.

twipper. to tremble: 'I come ower all of a twipper.' 2 to turn sharply and continuously. 3 to flicker.

twister. an unscrupulous person.

twitch. couch grass.

U

Words begining *un*, denoting contrary sense, are pronounced *on*.

ugly. unpleasant, repulsive, threatening.

ulve. see **elve**.

unkid, unky. ominous, uncanny. **unkid-an'-grievous,** strange and sad.

unsight-unseen. buying without inspecting.

up. full, complete: 'up (full) to the brim.' 2 to jump up: 'I ups and goos fer 'im.'

upland. high ground, slope of a hill. 2 country as opposed to town or village.

uppish. stuck-up.

uppity, uppety. proud.

upsidaisy, upadaisy. up again (in speaking to a child), up you go.

upsidown. down you go.

Market day at Hitchin: 'He useth to send hopps to market on the Lord's Day.'

up-so-down. upside down: 'The londe (land) was tourned up-so-down.' (Chaucer)

upsides with. to pay out, to be even with: 'I'll git upsides w'th 'im, see if I don't.'

upstreet, downstreet. up and down the village street.

up-top. at or on the top: 'Ye'll find it up top the cupboard.'

urchin. hedgehog: 'Paid for 1 urchin as I killed myself, 4d' (see **varmint**). See also **hedge'og**.

urgin. annoying: 'Now aint that urgin! Jist when I was set down t' me sewin'.'

urk, yark. strap or string round the leg to keep the trousers above the boot.

us. we: 'Where shall us lay him?' (Shakespeare, *Cymbeline IV.*2) 2 to me: 'Chuck us th' 'ammer.'

use. to accustom; 'Th' mare aint never carried a lady: we'll ev to use 'er to it.' 2 in the habit of: 'I didn' use ter.' '(He) useth to send hopps to market on the Lord's Day.' (Hert Sessions Rolls)

V

The initial letter V is usually pronounced like W.

wagabone, wagaborne. vagabond.

walley. valley.

wally. value.

wargin. virgin.

warmint. vermin: These were the fox, head-money 2s 6d; otter, 2s; polecat 4d; urchin (hedgehog), 2d; raven, 3d; bullfinch and kingfisher, 1d. 2 a term of affection: 'Come 'ere, ye little warmint you.''

vau't. vault: 'A vaught belonging to his Mansion House ... called la Falken Inn.' (Herts Sessions Rolls)

wentur. to venture.

Wer. the river Ver.

wery. very.

wex. to vex.

viage. voyage: 'He was late y-come from his viage.' (Chaucer, *Prologue*)

wi'lent. violent.

wi'lets. violets.

wisit. visit.

wittles. victuals: 'A meal o' wittles wou'nt coom amiss.' The old road men frequently used this term.

W

wad. a small portion of hay or straw.

wagin. wagon: 'as broad as a wagin wheel,' anything wide or large. Also said of dialect.

wallop. a hard blow: ''e did come down a wallop.'

walls, to lie by the walls. lying dead in the interval between death and burial.

wam'le. to wobble. **wam'ly, wambly,** wobbly: 'a bit wambly on me legs.'

want, went, wunt. a road; a four-want way, cross roads. 2 to be in need, to be without: 'Us wanted fer mos' ever'think.'

wanty, waanty, wunty. the strap or cord which passes under the horse and is secured to the shafts to prevent the cart from tilting when loaded. The wanty was originally the strap which secured the burden on a pack horse. 2 belly band.

waps, wapses. wasp, wasps. Wapses-neestes, wasps' nests.

war, wor, wor yow. beware, make way, look out.

warm. to thrash: 'Schoolmaster will warm 'e, no fear.'

warmint. see V.

wart charms. rub the warts with a black slug or with fig-leaves, bury the leaves in a dunghill; or cut as many notches in a stick of elder or thorn as there are warts; bury the stick in a bank. As the fig leaves or stick decay the warts disappear.

was to be, waant to be. fore-ordained, the will of God.

wash. a ford, or occasional flood.

waster. smut, see **thief**.

water-slade. a low-lying flat valley.

wattle and daub. wickerwork (plaited osier) plastered with clay and used for building.

way. away, do away with, to destroy.

way. road. 2 distance: 'Ye ev a goodish way ter goo yit.' 3 direction: 'I 'ould gi' 'e lift but I're gooin' Redb'n way.' 4 **driftway, drovers' road.** a way across country. 5 **fayring-way.**

a thoroughfare. 6 **market-way, pack and prime way.** packhorse way and original old track. 7 **purilly-way.** a path used in the perambulation of the parish bounds. 8 **rack-way.** a track through a wood. 9 **wicked way.** a rutty muddy lane. 10 **devil's way** and **twenty devils' way.** a practically impassable road. 11 **right of way.** lanes, bridle and footways belonging by usage to the people, and traversing private property.

we. us: 'It would a holp we fine.'

weather. 'Rain or fine we mun take th' weather as it cooms.' 'All weather is God's weather.' (Old sayings). Rainin', drizzlin', dampin' a bit, mistin', mizzlein'. spettin', spottin', wettin', now but a spirtle o' rain, a bit bashy or casalty, or soppin'-wet, a two-three heat-drops, etc. 'A bit black o-er Will's mother's way,' storm clouds in the west (origin unknown). 'Proper dark London way,' black clouds in the south.

weather-ear: "Unki'd day. Med (may) be gooin' ter ev a thun-er storm. Bes' kip yer weather-ear up.'

weather-eye. 'Kip yer weather-eye up.'

weeds: ''Twas th' deev'l as sowed 'em in 'arf'dsheer: thizzles an' nittles, darnock an' docks, cockledrakes, hawdoddles, kedlocks an' goolds, langley-beef, dog-fennel, deev'l's-guts, beggars'-lice an' a two-three 'underd moer.'

welcome. no thanks needed: 'Take some apples 'ome wuth 'e. You're welcome.'

well. interjection in common use at the beginning of a sentence.

well'igh, wellnigh. nearly. **well a nigh,** almost.

well away, well up in the boughs, well britched. fortunate, better off than other people.

wench. a girl. The wench and her chap, sweethearts. Going a-wenching, courting.

went. gone: 'Ef I'd a knowed in time I'd a went.' 2 been: "e aint went t' th' pub, p'or chap, fer a month o' Sundays.' 3 worked; 'That thar pump aint went tis two year an' moer.' 4 happened to, become of: 'What went on' the' snully-'orn cow?'

wer, war, wor, wus. was, were. **warnt, waunt,** was not, were not.

wer, er. our: 'Le's (lets) ev wer bevers.'

whack. a portion: 'Ther's yer whack an' ye ull git no mo.' 2 a hit: 'I fotch 'im a whack.'

The well known road-spanning inn sign of the Fox and Hounds at Barley: "e aint went t' th' pub, p'or chap, fer a month o' Sundays.'

whackin'. a beating.

whar, wher, wha-er, wheer. where: 'Whaer wus 'e?' 'Whar wer 'e? Why, ower thar.' 'Oh, ower tha'er.' ''ere or theer makes no odds.'

what. an interjection. 2 who: 'The chap what worked 'ere.'

what? what d'ye say? what siay? what by itself is considered unmannerly. **what yer arter?** What do you mean? **'I'll gi' 'e what fer,'** I'll punish you. **than what,** than: ''e's better off than what I be.' **but what,** but that: 'You can't lay down your umberella but what somebody will take it.' 'I can't believe but what he'll come.'

whatever. on any account, or at the end of a sentence for emphasis.

wheat-stitches. see **bout**.

wheedle. to obtain by flattery, or pertinacity: ''e'll do mer (more) ner wheedle! 'e'll ev yer.'

wheer. where, **somewheers,** somewhere.

whelm, whellum. also **cart-bridge,** a roughly made bridge for carts across a stream or ditch, sometimes made from one or more tree-trunks sawn in half lengthways, or hollowed out and used for a drain under or across a road leading from one field to another. 2 to cover one vessel with another or with a lid.

while. till: 'Bide 'ere while I get back' ... 'while sich time as I git 'ome frum work.'

whinnick. to whine or cry softly.

whinwhan. anything indescribable or for which the name is unknown.

whippersnapper. a small but active person: 'My noo daater'n-laa's a reglar lil whippersnapper, no bigger ner sixpen'orth o' coppers, but sharp as a needle.'

whippletree. the bar to which traces are fixed in horse harness.

whitchert. (white earth), used in building.

white hen's chicken. the favourite child of its mother.

whittle. to wear or fray by friction.

whoother. whether.

whop. to beat.

whopper. anything very large. **whopping,** very big.

whosen. whose.

wicker. willow.

wiggin'. a scolding.

wiggle. also **scriggle**, to wriggle, squirm.

wilk. to wilt. **wilked,** withered.

wind. to smell: 'Can't yer wind it? It stinks enough to knock yer back'ards.'

wissop. wisp: 'She looked like a drownded rat, the po'r lil wissop.'

wi'out, wuthouten, withouter, arout. without. 2 unless: 'I wunt let 'e goo without yer mother goos too.'

witch. The word witch, *wicca* (male), *wicce* (female), is from Old English *wiccian*, to practice witchcraft. There were witches of both sexes in Hertfordshire: black witches 'dealt in sorcery and enchantments, bewitching men and beasts, causing them to languish and die,' and white witches 'who set up to be respectable and to be of use to their neighbours,' who were supposed to be able – for a fee – to remove spells cast by black witches, to find lost or stolen property and by means of charms and secret remedies to cure the sick.

withy. willow. **withies**, osier rods used for hurdle and basket-making and for thatching roofs. See **wattle**.

wodehouse. a 'wild man,' who went round the village on Plow-Monday, as one of the mummers or Plow-Witches.

woll, wool, ool. will: 'I 'ool not be druv.'

won'erful. great (size, number).

wood. a wood may be a copse, frith or thrift, grove, hanger, holt, shaw, spinney, spring.

wooden head. an absent-minded person: 'Now then, wood'n 'ead, look wheer yer a-gooin'.'

wooden hill. the steep wooden stairs in cottages. 'Up the wooden hill to Bedfordshire.'

wooding. gathering sere wood.

wook. woke.

words, woords. a squabble: 'I wount ev no woords wi' 'e,' I tolt me neebour, 'but if the cap fits ee,' I tolt 'er, 'pull it well down.'

wore out. worn out. Also **tore out**.

work, woork. a fuss: 'Sech a woork as was made an' all o-er noothin'.'

workadays. weekdays: 'I wears me 'ob-nail boots a workadays, an me lahstic-sides a Sundays.'

worrit, werrit. to worry.

wraw. wrathful, angry.

wroot. to tear with the snout.

wrop. to wrap, wrapped.

wuman. woman: 'me ol' wuman,' my wife.

wus, wusser, wusserer. ill, worse: ''er wer taken wus in the night.'
  wust, worst.

     Beeswax an' turpentine,
     Thunder-pitch an' plaster,
     The more you try to pull it off
     The wus it sticks the faster. (Herts rhyme)

wuth. worth.

Y

yaller. yellow: 'Yer face is as yaller as a kite's foot.'

yammerin', complaining, jabbering.

yarbs. herbs.

yarn. earn

yarwig. earwig, see also **arwig**.

yawns. see **ails**.

ye, y', 'e, yer, yerself. you, your, yourself (singular and plural): 'Wull 'e do 't fer me?' 'Coom t' that, ye mout (might) do 't yerself.'

yea. yes, in answer to a direct question.

yelm, yolm. a portion of straightened straw handed to the thatcher by his boy.

yelm out. to lay the straw in one direction.

yelmin', yollermin'. preparing the straw for thatching or hay for cutting into chaff.

yelp. to boast, prate: 'I keep noght of armes for to yelp' (no arms to boast of). (Chaucer, Knight's Tale)

yesemaker. see **saye**.

yoffle. to eat greedily and noisily.

yoll, yoller. to yell, holloa: 'I yoller'd 'im t' goo tother way.'

yolp. to gulp.

yommick. see **ommick**.

yong, yoong. young: 'A yong Squyer' (squire). (Chaucer, *Prologue*)

yorks. strap or string below knee to keep trousers up.

yorp. to make a noise: 'A done now, do! Stop yorpin'.'

you. used for emphasis and at the end of a sentence: 'Y' little mischief, you.'

yowe. ewe: 'old yowe done up lamb fashion,' a woman dressed too young for her age.

yulk. yolk.